EURO

German Conservative Foreign Policy 1870-1940

SELECTED READINGS

Translated with an Introduction and Notes by

Alexander Jacob

University Press of America,® Inc.
Lanham · New York · Oxford

Copyright © 2001 by
University Press of America,® Inc.
4720 Boston Way
Lanham, Maryland 20706
UPA Acquisitions Department (301) 459-3366

12 Hid's Copse Rd.
Cumnor Hill, Oxford OX2 9JJ

Library of Congress Cataloging-in-Publication Data

Europa : German conservative foreign policy, 1870-1940 : selected
readings / translated with an introduction and notes by Alexander Jacob.
      p.   cm
"This edition is ... a supplement to ... Edgar Julius Jung's Die
Herrschaft der Minderwertigen ... published by the Edwin Mellen Press,
Lewiston, NY, 1995"—P.v.
Includes bibliographical references and index.
1. Germany—Foreign relations—1871-1918. 2. Germany—Foreign
relations—1918-1933. 3. Conservatism—Germany—History. 4. National
socialism. 5. Antisemitism—Germany—History. 6. State, The.
7. Conservatism—Europe—History. 8. Nationalism—Europe—
History. 9. Nationalism—Germany—History. I. Jacob, A. (Alexander)
II. Jung, Edgar J. (Edgar Julius), 1894-1934. Herrschaft der
Minderwertigen, ihr Zerfall und ihre Ablösung.

DD221 .E9 2001   327.43'009'034—dc21   2001053077 CIP

ISBN 0-7618-2137-6 (pbk. : alk. paper)

Contents

Acknowledgements

This edition is in many respects a supplement to my translation of Edgar Julius Jung's *Die Herrschaft der Minderwertigen*, which was published by the Edwin Mellen Press, Lewiston, NY, 1995. Since I omitted in that translation some of the chapters related to foreign policy, I am glad that the present edition provides a fuller view of Jung's foreign political considerations. In addition, the placing of Jung's work within a context of German political philosophy from the Second Reich onwards should help the reader to obtain a more comprehensive understanding of the major themes of Conservative German foreign policy which prevailed till the end of the Third Reich.

I should like to thank Frau Christa Spangenberg, née Jung, and Joachim Jung, of Munich, for their kind consent to publish these translations from their father's work. Since Part I, Ch.X and Part VI, Chapters, 5, 8, 9, 10, of Jung's work have already appeared in my edition, *The Rule of the Inferiour*, I should like to thank the Edwin Mellen Press for permission to reproduce these sections here. Finally, I should thank the Department of Political Science at the University of Toronto for the Fellowship that I held there during the composition of this work.

Toronto   Alexander Jacob

Introduction

I have sought in this edition to present to the modern reader four major German thinkers spanning the crucial historical period from 1870 to the second world war in the hope of revealing the spiritual and cultural motives that inspired the German conservative mind in its effort to redeem Europe from the social dangers besetting the European peoples. The history of the idea of a consolidated `Mitteleuropa' dates back to the economists Friedrich List and Freiherr von Bruck, though their proposals were mostly focussed on the economic benefits to be derived from a closer association between the Prussian and the Austrian Reichs.[1] It was Paul de Lagarde and Constantin Frantz who first presented what may be called a philosophical argument for a reorganisation of Europe on the basis of a strong Germanic central Europe. The notion of a federalistic European Reich was continued in the work of the Weimar Neoconservative, Edgar Julius Jung, while the Nazi ideologue Rosenberg reinterpreted this political theme as a contest of racial worth on the European mainland.[2]

---

1 For a survey of the history of `Mitteleuropa', see J. Stern, `*Mitteleuropa' von Leibniz bis Naumann über List und Frantz, Planck und Lagarde*, Stuttgart: Deutsche Verlagsanstalt, 1917, H.C. Meyer, *Mitteleuropa in German thought and action 1815-1945*, The Hague: Martinus Nijhoff, 1955 and J. Droz, *L'Europe centrale: évolution historique de l'idée de `Mitteleuropa'*, Paris: Payot, 1960.

2 I do not consider Friedrich Naumann's major work, *Mitteleuropa* (1915), which enjoyed a great success at the time of its publication since, in spite of its apparent revival of the idea of the Holy Roman Empire, it is basically Liberal in character and ingenuously believes that Jews are important for the development of Europe,

The inclusion of Alfred Rosenberg should serve to highlight the fact that National Socialism was in many respects a practical manifestation of conservative aspirations in a time of extreme social and economic crisis. The centrality of the Jewish question in discussions of the reorganisation of Europe is also evident in the political writings of all the thinkers presented here. The lack of German translations of these important texts so far has clearly been a disadvantage to the modern historian in his assessment of the philosophical significance of the conservative, as well as of the National Socialist, foreign political ideology. Of the four thinkers chosen in this edition, two, i.e. Lagarde and Jung, are professed Conservatives, while Frantz's conservatism is subsumed by his system of European 'federalism' and Rosenberg's by his all-encompassing 'racialism'.

Paul de Lagarde (1827-1891)

Paul Anton Bötticher (later called Paul de Lagarde) was born in Berlin in 1827 and did his doctorate at the University of Berlin before becoming an instructor at the Friedrich-Werderschen Gymnasium. In 1867 a grant from the King allowed him to retire to Schleusingen to conduct his scholarly theological and orientalistic researches for a year. He received no university position until 1869 in the Georgia Augusta Universität in Göttingen. His later years at Göttingen were marked by the publication of several political essays which crystallised his radical conservative views. Lagarde's criticisms of Bismarck's Reich were similar to Frantz's since both perceived the innate tendency towards parliamentarism and particularism in Bismarck's plans as a deleterious contribution to the essentially conservative tradition of Germany. Bismarck's indifference to foreign policy was also a disappointment to Lagarde's colonial desires. Besides, the decisive reforms in education and Church organisation that Lagarde insisted on were not carried through by the new Reich. Lagarde's most important work in this period was the *Über die gegenwärtige Lage des deutschen Lage des deutschen Reichs* (1875) which consisted of a detailed critique of every aspect, social, economic, cultural and political, of the Reich. In 1878 Lagarde published his political and religious writings in a collection called the *Deutsche Schriften* which enjoyed

---

especially Eastern Europe, because of their economic power.

considerable popularity in Germany. In 1881 a second volume of essays was added to the *Deutsche Schriften* and the two volumes were later, in 1886, collected into a single volume, along with three new essays, including the `Programm für die Konservative Partei Preussens'. This essay, as Lougee points out, "anticipated the conservative revolution of the twentieth century".[3] Lagarde's vision of a renewed conservative idealism as the true basis of German politics was vigorously acclaimed both by conservatives like Thomas Mann (in his essay, `Die Politik' in *Betrachtungen eines Unpolitischen* (1918)) and Edgar Julius Jung (in his conservative treatise, *Die Herrschaft der Minderwertigen* (1929, 1930)) and by Nazi intellectuals like Alfred Rosenberg (in his essay, "Paul de Lagarde und die Banken", *Völkischer Beoabchter*, 8 May, 1921, and in his major work, *Der Mythus des 20. Jahrhunderts*, Bk.III, Ch.I).

Although Lagarde supplied the intellectual foundations for a true Conservative political system in Germany, he refused all invitations to participate in politics or polemics. He refused even to participate in a periodical for Richard Wagner and his ideas just as he avoided all involvement in Theodor Fritsch's Antisemitic movement. Lagarde's conservatism was based on the Idealistic notion of the primacy of the individual spirit or personality as the divine spark in man which corresponded in the social sphere to the `nation' as opposed to the `state'. The nation is an organism and can flourish only on the basis of commonalty of spiritual concerns rather than the divisive principle of material interest. His criticisms of dogmatic religion, whether Protestant or Catholic, were directed by the concern to propagate true metaphysical feeling or piety as the religious foundation of the nation. Germany especially has a greater responsibility to maintain this religious spirit since it alone of the modern Indo-European races is a young, or "original", race and still in contact with its original ethos.

Lagarde's radical conservatism necessarily revolved around the idea of the monarchy since only a German monarch could, as the representative of God, preserve the German spirit as well as the German people who are, indeed, a particular `thought' of God. The monarch must be supported by a strong, regenerated aristocracy which would assure the freedom of the people from oppressive government. The people should be granted a certain degree of representation but not in the foolish way of

---

3 Robert W. Lougee, *Paul de Lagarde 1827-1891: A study of radical conservatism in Germany*, Cambridge, MA: Harvard University Press, 1962, p.108.

voting. Rather they should express the "folk will" that would override the partisan special interests which would otherwise control legislation. This can be effected through the admission of representatives of the people to approve or reject laws created by a legislative council of experts in the several fields of government, such as finance or military affairs. In the 'Programm' Lagarde suggested that it were better if the membership of the people in the Landtag and the Reichstag were restricted to the communal estates and the local chambers of commerce while the higher assemblies consisted of men more experienced in local affairs. Bureaucrats are, in all cases, to be excluded from such participation. In his essay of 1885, *Die nächsten Pflichten deutscher Politik*, Lagarde included the higher ranks of the nobility in the assemblies which are to be formed in an *ad hoc* manner to decide on specific social issues.[4]

Lagarde's conservatism necessarily involved the idea of a return to a mediaeval system of society and politics which in turn finds its fullest expression in the revival of a Holy Roman Empire of the German Nation. Germany must become the leader again of the Central European land mass organized as a *pax germanica*. He was not in favour of Bismarck's Prussianization of Germany and proposed instead a dualistic greater Germany focussed in Austria as well as in Prussia. In his essay, *Über die gegenwärtigen Aufgaben der deutschen Politik* (1853), Lagarde included in his greater Germany the states of the Confederation along with Hungary and Galicia, Venice and Lombardy, so that Mitteleuropa would extend from "the Danish frontier in the northwest, south to --- most of the valleys of the Moselle and the Saar, northeast to the marshes of eastern Poland, and southeast to the Black Sea and the Adriatic".[5] Unlike Frantz, Lagarde did not envisage regional autonomy to all nationalities within the Central European territory since he considered the Hungarians, Czechs and South Slavs as a "burden on history" which could perform a good service only "as an alloy with nobler metal".[6] Germany would be assured of food, political strength, and spiritual culture only within such a broad territory and the old dynastic families, such as the Reuss, Lippes, Solms, could reassume their historic functions as heriditary rulers of the Danubian lands. The deplorable loss of Germans through emigration to America can be fruitfully counteracted by diverting this emigration to the

---

4 This plan for *ad hoc* councils of experts is repeated by Chamberlain in his *Politische Ideale* (München, 1915).

5 Lougee, *op.cit.*, p.186.

6 'Aufgaben' in *Deutsche Schriften*, Göttingen, 1886, p.34.

neighbouring lands of Central Europe. After the formation of the Reich in 1871, Lagarde began to consider Russia as the principal danger to Germany being, as he expressed it, a monstrosity constituted of "Catholicism, Judaism, and North America wrapped into one". Since by 1890 France too turned towards Russia, and England had forfeited its role as a continental power through its perfidious transactions, only Germany now could ensure the moral and political safety of Europe threatened by Russia on the one side and America on the other.

Throughout his career, Lagarde identified the Jews as an alien nation within the European nations and as a thoroughly deleterious one since it was synonymous with Liberalism and capitalism and the other forces which inexorably erode the spiritual core of the European peoples. In the 'Programm' Lagarde recognizes the parasitical nature of the Jews and the danger of their assuming high positions in finance, politics, and education. Through their traditional usurious occupations they have now unfortunately achieved world power. Yet surprisingly, Lagarde did not recommend any extreme measures against the Jews and hoped that if they could not be forced to leave Germany altogether they could at least be Germanized. The chief distinction of Lagarde's conception of the new greater Germany is that it is based on a spiritual understanding of the racial bases of the nation, where the excellence of the German races is to be safeguarded by a social and geographical reorganisation of Europe against the Liberal threats to them presented by the Jewish and Jewish-influenced elements of Europe as well as by the lesser races, such as mainly the Russian.

In the excerpts presented in this edition from Lagarde's 'Programm für die Konservative Partei Preussens', we note immediately the true monarchical condition of Conservatism as well the organic nature of its social organisation. German colonialism is vigorously encouraged by Lagarde, with Austria considered as an indispensable extension of German national culture. The Jews themselves are opposed to national culture (as distinct from national *states*) and must be removed unless they, in exceptional cases, reveal themselves to be truly inclined to become Germanized. This latter possibility would naturally entail also the resolve of the Germans to remain truly German themselves.

Constantin Frantz (1817-1891)

Constantin Frantz was less nationalistic than his contemporary

Lagarde and his major ideal of European federalism was based less on spiritual and racial supports than Lagarde's plans for a Germanic Central Europe. In spite of his Schellingian affiliations, Frantz's idea of European federalism as a response to the growing Liberal tendency towards nationalistic particularism in Europe was not inspired by an understanding of the special value of the German spirit so much as by a conventional Christian notion of the brotherhood of men.[7] Frantz began his academic career with the publication of studies on the philosophy of mathematics and Hegelianism, which he soon renounced, and critiques of the systems of Friedrich Strauss and Ludwig Feuerbach. His major study of Schelling's philosophy was published as *Schellings positive Philosophie* (3 vols., Köther, 1880). His political interests began with his career as secretary to various politicians and diplomats, and, in 1846, he published a study on *The Present and Future of the Prussian Constitution*, which was followed in 1850 by a pamphlet on *Our Policy*. Although as a result of his diplomatic experiences he was offered the Consulate-General at Smyrna and at Galatz, as well as later the Chairmanship at the University of Breslau, he refused these positions in favour of his own independent work, which he continued to publish from Berlin and Blasewitz. His major works of the last period were *Der Föderalismus als leitende Prinzip für die soziale, staatliche und internationale Organisation* (München, 1879) and *Die Weltpolitik unter besonderer Bezugnahme auf Deutschland* (Chemnitz, 1882).

Frantz's political system is a consistent criticism of the Bismarckian, since he recognized in the latter the same defects which Bismarck was apparently attacking in the Liberal and Socialist groups, both of which are supported on the false foundations of Hegelian rationalism, which is a mockery of true Idealism. Bismarck's glorification of Prussia is detrimental to the rest of Germany, which should be guaranteed the rights of regional autonomy.[8] The centralisation and uniformity which Bismarck championed are dangerous since Prussia, which bears the weight of such a centralisation, is rapidly developing into a French-style militaristic state. Frantz particularly opposes the Reich's callous attitude

---

7 In this notion of federalism based on the Christian brotherhood of man, Frantz was influenced by the work of Adam Müller (1779-1826), whose idea of a federation of nations was inspired by the Christian "Gemeinschaft der Heiligen" (see Müller, *Die Elemente der Staatskunst*, 1809 [ed. J. Baxa, Jena: G. Fischer, 1922]).

8 cf. his *Der dänische Erbfolgstreit und die Bundespolitik* (Berlin, 1864).

to ethnic minorities such as the Poles who should have been supported by Germany as a common friend against the Russians.

Frantz's view of the future Germany is decidedly `grossdeutsch' and therefore critical of Bismarck's exclusion of Austria from the Reich. In his *Polen, Preussen und Deutschland,* Frantz urged a synthesis of Great German and Lesser German tendencies to form a Central European Reich which would serve as an intermediary between nations. Poland, in particular, should not be Germanized. In his next works, *Die deutsche Föderation* (Leipzig, 1851), and *Untersuchungen über das europäische Gleichgewicht* (Berlin, 1859), he proposed the pan-German idea of a union between Prussia and Austria. He believed that England would be a natural ally of this Central European alliance, which would aim at counteracting the Franco-Russian alliance. France, as a champion of nationalism and national states, is too materialistic and atheistic to be integrated into Mitteleuropa, just as Russia is too schismatic. In his *Die Wiederherstellung Deutschlands* (Berlin, 1856), Frantz proposed a double confederation, one in the west which would encompass the solely German states, that is, the provinces west of the Elbe in Prussia and, in Austria, the Tyrol, the Vorarlberg, and Salzburg; the other a looser one encompassing all the other Prussian and Austrian states such as Bohemia and Galicia.

Internationally, too, the new conditions of a world-economy demand the imposition of a federalistic organisation of states. Perennially hostile states like Russia, however, can be forced to adopt the new system only by conquest. Thus, while Frantz is generally a Christian pacifist, he is not opposed to the use of violence in the case of recalcitrant forces. The great-power system must be destroyed forthwith since its hegemonistic tendencies are precisely a hindrance to the fraternal bases of federalism. Whereas Jung's federalistic system is a more thoroughly neo-mediaeval one that is formed in an organic manner with Germany as its spiritual core, Frantz proposes a "federation of independent members, and that with a polyglot formation, in opposition to the universal Latinism of the Middle Ages".[9] However, in spite of Frantz's frequent recourse to Christian feeling as a support of his political system, he does not envisage the future federalistic Europe as a republican or parliamentary one but as one based on authority, even monarchical, a fact which highlights the Conservative basis of his thought. In his monarchism, Frantz is again opposed to Bismarck who favoured the unnatural system of a

---

9 cf. p.81 below.

constitutional monarchy. The parliamentary system must be replaced by a corporative one constituted of delegates from the big state social and economic bodies. The universities should be expressly excluded from participation in political affairs since Frantz (like Eugen Dühring his contemporary)[10] recognized the lack of independent thought in the typical university professor.

The Central European federation that is proposed by Frantz in *Der Föderalismus* obviously does not include France, whose rationalistic flavour is too nationalistic, or Spain and Italy, which are stuck in their splendid past, or Russia, which is hardly European but an alloy of "the cunning of the Mongols and the Western *savoir-faire*".[11] In spite of his original respect for England, Frantz realizes now that even England's role in history has been mostly an extra-continental one and cannot be included in the Central European federation. So, only Germany is qualified to be a leader in the new federal Europe, since she has not only provided the heads of the most of the major dynasties of Europe but her own national constitution has always been essentially a federalistic one right from the time of the Holy Roman Empire of the German Nation. Germany should strive consistently for the restraining of barbaric Russia from interfering in European affairs and this check can be effected only by encouraging Prussia's traditional historical `Drang nach Osten' with a justified use of force. Only then will Russia begin to realize that her mission is towards Asia and the Mongol menace and not towards Europe. It is one of Frantz's major merits that he, like Lagarde, foresaw the political influence of Russia as well as that of the U.S.A. as being the major future threats to the stability of his federal Central Europe. The federation of Europe as envisaged by Frantz will consist of two major monarchies, the Prussian and the Austrian, around which will be grouped the south-German states, the Alemannic federation and the Grand-Duchy of Luxembourg. Switzerland, Belgium and Holland must sooner or later be admitted into the Central European federation. The Scandinavian states could form a *Territorium* or sub-federation. The Papacy should be transferred to Jerusalem, and Catholicism, severed from its present Roman affiliations, will be made a universal institution once again constituted of a federation of all the diverse confessions that at present tear Christianity apart.

Bismarck's Christianity is a mere façade since it is narrowly

---

10 cf. p.100n. below.
11 Sauzin, *op.cit.*, 132.

nationalistic and lacks the true Christian feeling of brotherhood which can be fostered only under a federalistic system. Federalism is firmly opposed to Socialism, which wishes foolishly to be free of the past, and even to Conservatism insofar as the latter is often too restrictedly bound to the past. Federalism is an organic (Schellingian) system which assures what Sauzin summarizes as "continuity of evolution, action of the parts on the whole and of the whole on the parts". Rationalism and humanism are the two major evils which have spawned nationalism and socialism which in turn have destroyed Europe's traditional mediaeval hierarchical and monarchical society. These two blemishes in the aspect of European politics are embodied in the Jewish race, which are the most harmful to a federalistic organisation of Europe since they are determined not to participate in European culture but to rule the divided states of Europe through their financial hegemony. The emancipation of the Jews was the greatest error of European politics since they have now become able to infiltrate all the more easily the higher echelons of trade, the stock-exchange, the press, the universities and the organs of culture, and even the Reichstag. The Jews should be deported *en masse* to Palestine if they are not sooner or later to face the rage of the exploited Europeans.

Frantz does not seem to have arrived at Dühring's understanding of the Jewish problem as a racial rather than a religious one and believing that "among the Jews, nationality and religion are inseparably one", it is enough if they "first give up their religion in order to be able to lay aside their nationality and become indeed real Germans".[12] His focus on the Jewish question is predominantly oriented to the commercial aspect of the Jewish life which seeks to profit from the labour of the host nations. The freedom of vocation acquired by the Jews through their emancipation has allowed them to penetrate into the leading positions in the press, stock-exchange, education and even politics. For, the Jews are an exploitative group not only nationally but also internationally. This international system of wealth is facilitated by the scattered situation of the Jews all over the world and by the fact that the traditional intermarriage of the Jews among themselves has ensured that "the wealth acquired by Jews also remains always within the circle of the same".[13] The solution to the Jewish problem lies in the issuing of exceptional laws with regard to the Jews, just as the remedy for the Jewish supra-national rule is the federalistic organisation of the world. The existing great power

---

12 cf. p.59 below.
13 cf. p.57 below.

system is one based on military might, which is only the political counterpart of the financial rule both representing empty power. Only a federalistic organisation of Europe can assure the autonomy of the smaller states at the same time as it organically fosters the cultural development of the various nations.

Edgar Julius Jung (1894-1934)

Conservative and federalistic views unite in the thought of the leading Neo-Conservative theorist of the Weimar Republic, Edgar Julius Jung. Jung was not only a political thinker and propagandist but also an active politician in the Weimar Republic, having begun his political career simultaneously with his legal practice soon after the first World War. Jung was born in 1894 in the Bavarian Palatinate and served as a volunteer in the war.[14] After the war, he joined a Free Corps unit and participated in the liberation of Munich from the Bavarian Soviet Republic in the spring of 1919. Before the Franco-Belgian occupation of the Ruhr (1923-25), Jung had completed his doctorate in law and began practice in Zweibrücken. His political activities during this time included organizing terrorist resistance activities against the Ruhr occupation and serving on the directory of the Deutsche Volkspartei. After the Ruhr crisis, Jung established himself as an attorney in Munich where he lived until his death. Jung was a member of the neoconservative Juniklub and its successor, the Herrenklub, and acquired reknown through his several political writings in the *Deutsche Rundschau*, as well as through the *Herrschaft*, which, according to Jean Neuhrohr, was a sort of "bible of neoconservatism".[15]

---

14 I am indebted for much of my information regarding Jung's political career to Larry Eugene Jones' two significant articles on Jung, "Edgar Julius Jung: The Conservative Revolution in theory and practice", *Central European History*, 21 (1988), pp.142-74, and "The limits of collaboration: Edgar Jung, Herbert von Bose, and the origins of the Conservative resistance to Hitler, 1933-34" in L.E. Jones and J. Retallack (ed.), *Between Reform, Reaction, and Resistance: Studies in the History of German Conservatism from 1789 to 1945*, Oxford and Providence, R.I.: Berg Publishers, 1993, pp.465-501.
15 Jean F. Neurohr, *Der Mythos vom 3. Reich: Zur Geistesgeschichte des Nationalsozialismus*, Stuttgart, 1957, p.187 (cf. W.Struve, *Elites against*

In January 1930, Jung joined the Volkskonservative Vereinigung, a right-wing party formed initially by twelve Reichstag deputies who had seceded from the Deutschnationale Volkspartei led by Alfred Hugenberg. Jung's attitude to the rising National Socialist party of Hitler was lukewarm, since, in spite of his admiration of the "positive energies" of the movement, he considered it to be only an extreme form of Liberalism. partisan political life, were prepared to look at contemporary political problems from the sole perspective of the historical mission of the German people".[16] However, Jung's refusal to co-operate with the more derate Conservatives like Heinrich Brüning[17] and G.R. Treviranus, in order to promote his own brand of revolutionary conservatism, did not help his movement, which lost virtually all political force by the Spring of 1931.

When Hitler and the National Socialist party gained massive victories in the state and regional elections of 24 April, 1932, Jung actually welcomed the legal accession of the Nazis to power. For, although Jung was still apprehensive of the extremist tendencies of the Nazis, he hoped that this legal process would obviate a forced seizure which would be a greater political "debacle". Besides, the tide of Nazi enthusiasm in the country was unstoppable and the Conservative alliance merely looked on helplessly as the NSDAP won a resounding victory in the Reichstag election of November 1932. Jung was naturally surprised when Hitler shrewdly joined forces with the Conservative Franz von Papen to form a coalition government in January 1933.

Jung had always maintained a superior attitude to Hitler's populism, and believed that, since the Conservatives were "responsible that this guy

---

Democracy, Princeton, NJ: Princeton University Press, 1973, p.321).

16 Vorbreitender Ausschuss der Volkskonservativen Bewegung zu deutscher Erneuerung, `Aufruf!', Bundesarchiv: ZSg 1-275/1 (The translation is that of L.E. Jones, "Edgar Julius Jung", p.156).

17 Jung's lack of enthusiasm for the Brüning chancellorship was explained by him in a draft of a letter to Brüning appended to a letter to Pechel dated 14 August 1931: "Only when the government is well on its way to returning to the concept of authority and to freeing itself from the sterility of German parliamentarism can these forces be placed in the service of the nation as a whole. In reorganizing the cabinet the goal should be the complete abandonment of its party basis. Not the approval of parties, but professional and practical competence should determine the selection of those whom you, respected chancellor, will need to help you in the mastery of these difficult tasks."

came to power; now we have to get rid of him".[18] So, when Papen was appointed vice chancellor after Brüning, in 1933, Jung wrote to Papen offering his services as a speech writer and intellectual advisor. On the advice of his close associate, Hans Haumann, Papen invited Jung to join his government in an advisory and organisatory capacity. Jung's intention in serving the Papen administration was "to surround [Papen] with a wall of conservatives" who would provide the vice-chancellor with the required moral fortification against Hitler's rapid rise to power.[19] Hoping to restrain the extremism of Hitler with his Conservative ideology, Jung served as speech-writer for Papen when Papen, Hugenberg and Franz Seldte of the Stalhelm joined to form the conservative Kampfront Schwarz-Weiss-Rot. His speeches were all designed to impress the new coalition of right-wing forces with a Conservative stamp rather than an extremist Nazi one. Jung defended the Papen government against the Nazis' accusations of reactionarism by stressing the revolutionary nature of the new Right and highlighting the spiritual and ideological defects of Hitler and his party.

While Papen endeavoured to combat the Nazi movement from a Conservative standpoint, Jung wrote a critique of the Nazi phenomenon in his *Sinndeutung der deutschen Revolution* (1933), which reiterated his accusations of Liberalism and democratism while stressing that "the aim of the national revolution must be the depoliticization of the masses and their exclusion from the leadership of the state". Jung called for a new state based on religion and a universalist world-view. Not the masses but a new nobility, or a self-conscious elite, should inform the new government, and Christianity must be the moral force behind the state. Society itself must be organized hierarchically and beyond the confines of nationalism even though it should be based on "an indestructible völkisch foundation from which the völkisch struggle can form".[20] The reference to going beyond the limits of Nationalism was of course prompted by his desire to reinstitute a federalistic pan-European Reich. Jung's Conservatism was also distinguished by its call for the creation of an elective monarchy and the appointment of an imperial regent as the

---

18 Remark to Rudolf Pechel, Jan.30, 1933, quoted in Jones, *op.cit.*, p.160.
19 See Jung's letter to Rudolf Pechel, 1 Feb. 1933, referred to in L.E. Jones, "Limits of Collaboration", p.475.
20 Manuscript of a lecture entitled "Sinndeutung der konservativen Revolution in Deutschland", University of Zürich, 7 Feb., 1934 (cited from Jones, `Edgar Julius Jung', p.167).

focus of the new Germanic European Reich.[21] But both the project of the Reich and the emphasis on völkisch foundations were carried out more dramatically, if rashly, by Hitler than any Conservative leaders could do.

Jung's opposition to Hitler took a more concerted form in early 1934 when he undertook extensive travels throughout Germany to develop a network of Conservative supporters who would assist in overthrowing the Hitler regime. Papen himself was unaware of Jung's efforts in this direction and Jung's chief assistance came from Herbert von Bose, Günther von Tschirschky, and Ketteler. Jung even contemplated personally assassinating Hitler,[22] though fears that this drastic action might disqualify him from assuming a leading role in the new leadership after the Nazi dictatorship caused him to adopt the academic alternative of writing another speech for Papen which the latter delivered at the University of Marburg on 17 June, 1934. The repeated attacks on the illegitimacy of the Hitler regime and the practical political failures of this regime in this speech forced Hitler, under counsel from Göring, Himmler and his assistant Heydrich, to get rid of the menace posed by Jung. Thus, along with Röhm and the SA officers who had become rebellious, Jung too lost his life in the "Night of the long knives", on 30 June, 1934.

Jung's Conservatism is at once national cultural and universalistic. Jung begins his *Herrschaft* with the negative ideal of individualism which characterizes the French Revolutionary Liberal ethic and then goes on to portray the truly German, organic, form of the state. The pseudo-philosophical concepts of *fraternité*, *liberté*, and *egalité* are recognized as being basically rationalistic and individualistic and fully opposed to the truly metaphysical instinct of the Germans, which is based on the intuition of the suprasensual, transcendent realm of the Divine. Whereas the individualist calls for fraternity, or universal suffrage, the truly philosophical person considers the welfare of the community (Gemeinschaft). Similarly, Jung decries the democratic notion of liberty as egotism derived from a matter-oriented understanding and one ignorant of the true spiritual freedom of the fully realized personality.

21 Denkschrift Edg. Jungs an Papen, April 1934, ACDP, Nachlass Forschbach, I-199/104/2 (see Jones, *op.cit.*, p.168).
22 Jung had earlier assisted in the plot to assassinate Franz Josef Heinz-Orbis, the president of the Autonomous Republic of the Palatinate, a separatist state supported by French conspiracy (see F. Grass, "Edgar Julius Jung", *Pfälzer Lebensbilder*, I (1964), pp.324-28).

The Liberal notion of `freedom' is typified by self-will, whereas true freedom is indeed "the creative power towards the divine life" arising from a consciousness of the unity of all the individual parts in an organic social and political whole. As for equality, it is "that political plague of the west"[23] which forms not a real community (Gemeinschaft) but only an artificial society (Gesellschaft),[24] for the former is always based on a hierarchical ranking of its members.

The individualism which impelled the French Revolution in fact began to emerge in Western history from the end of the Middle Ages, that is, the early Renaissance. The increasing commercialisation and bourgeois nature of society led to, first, Liberal and, then, Communistic and Nationalistic modes of political thought. The loss of the sense of spiritual values and worth has detracted from the realisation of the higher spiritual potential of man and led to the disappearance of religion. The emphasis on `human rights' rather than human worth has also produced a softening of character and the dull pacifistic mentality among politicians. The Germans, who are the centre of Europe geographically and spiritually, must reverse this trend since they alone are capable of forming an organic community based on the soil and the blood and characterised by a devotion to metaphysical ideals and a will to self-sacrifice. The religious sense must be revived in a regenerated Christianity which is at once Protestant and Catholic in the original sense of both these terms.

In a democracy, the common man, characterized by resentment of all forms of superiority, perpetuates the rule of mediocrity. By granting equal rights to all and sundry, democracy will lead to a chaos of mutually opposed individuals, that is, to total anarchy. Self-interest takes the form of material interests, and economic values predominate to the extent that "financial pirates" manipulate the entire institution of democracy through political parties. Jung does not stress race as a factor of national development as much as the `völkisch' thinkers of the National Socialist movement since eugenics seemed to him a materialisation of racialism, which should be based on spiritual qualities and not on blood.[25] But on

---

23 The `west' was the customary form of reference to the Revolutionary politics emanating from France.
24 These terms are borrowed from Ferdinand Tönnies' *Gemeinschaft und Gesellschaft: Grundbegriffe der reinen Soziologie*, Berlin, 1912.
25 Jung's discussion of the question of race is to be found in Part V of his book (which deals with population policy), especially Ch.8.

this spiritual basis, even if not on that of biological purity, even Jung distinguishes the Jews as a deleterious race devoted to individualism and its social variants, Liberalism and artificial `collectivism':

> It is correct that the Jews inhabit predominantly the camp of individualism. Seen from the standpoint of this book, they are reactionaries who, by and large, hold fast to a world-view which must be overcome. The Jews are individualistic and thereby the people of collectivism. They have little understanding of the Faustian battle for inner freedom. The heroic as well as the tragic does not find a place in them - not considering the heroic attitude of many individuals. The idea of immortality, a demand of the practical reason in Kant, is transferred, among the Jews, from the metaphysical to the this-worldly.[26]

The Jews have gained the ascendancy in the course of the periods of cultural degeneration which mark the modern history of the West. The Germans have subjected themselves to the commercial `spirit of the age' so much that they stand in the danger of being repressed once again by their adoption of "the manner and method of the Jewish people".[27] It is the duty of the nation to preserve the best type of races, even if mixed, and to deter the worse. And this can be accomplished only if the Germans themselves turn away from individualistic ways of thought and develop their spiritual and organic capacities as a community.

True Conservatism is therefore the cultivation of the true spiritual worth of a people and the necessary destruction of worthlessness as a revolutionary prerequisite for the accomplishment of this goal. In this context, it may be pointed out that, although Jung's attitude to the Jews is not as extreme as that of the National Socialists, the recognition of individualism as the chief ill of western society, as well as the identification of the Jews as the typical individualists, makes his entire work an anti-Semitic political treatise. The only difference between his system and the Nazi movement's focus on the Jews is that, having posited the hierarchical organisation of society according to individual merit, he did not have to advocate the forcible removal of the Jews from German society.

Given the universalistic nature of the neo-mediaeval Reich that

---

26 cf. p.97 below.
27 cf. p.101 below.

Jung sought to revive, it is not surprising that pride of place in his Conservative treatise, *Die Herrschaft der Minderwertigen* is given to foreign policy. For the true value of a nation is expressed in its dealings with other nations. The inequality of individuals also betokens, on a larger political scale, the inequality of nations. While individualism considers nations in terms of economic internationalism and colonial imperialism, the organic nation organises them in a federalistic, or autonomous, manner with leadership granted to the most spiritually advanced nation. As Germany is superior to all others in its metaphysical quality, it should conduct the spiritual revival of Europe. In this Jung is similar to a number of other German nationalistic thinkers from Fichte and Chamberlain to Moeller van den Bruck and the National Socialists, who insisted that it was the duty of Germany to ennoble the world. Jung's foreign policy is directed, like the rest of his political project, by the difference between individualism and concern for the national community. He considers the decline of Germany's situation in Europe as being due to the ascendancy of France, along with its individualistic polity, from the Renaissance onwards. The remedy for Germany's lost glory in Europe is the restoration of her people to the centre of the political life of the continent on a federative basis. The European federation must be ruled by Germany, exactly as in the mediaeval 'Holy Roman Empire of the German Nation'. Not only Austria but all the other border areas which have a considerable number of Germans in them should be merged with the German nation.

Projects put forward at the time by other federalists are inadequate since they are based on a blind desire for equality and freedom so that they only seek to "transform the whole of Europe into a gigantic mass democracy". The plans for a Pan-Europe put forward by Count Nikolaus von Coudenhove-Kalergi (1894-1972) in Vienna are untenable as well, since they not only accede to the artificial economic divisions of the Versailles Treaty but also focus on Russia as the main centre of the European problem. Jung, with greater foresight, sees the Russian question as dependent on the German since the latter is more important spiritually as well as geographically and the reorganisation of Europe must necessarily begin with Prussia rather than Russia. Besides, the system of Count Nikolaus, himself the hybrid progeny of an Austrian aristocrat and a Japanese woman, makes the terrible mistake of ignoring the importance of racial values in envisioning a future Europe characterised by an Eurasiatic-Negroid race and led by the Jews. The support that France and the Berlin banks, especially, have given Coudenhove's plans is confirmation of Jung's observations on the defective character of French polity as well as of German Liberalism. Coudenhove's plan for Pan-Europe envisages all the democratic nations of Europe in a federation of 26 larger states and 7 smaller territories with 300 million inhabitants - a monstrosity that is ridiculed by Jung as "superimperialistic formal democracy with all the mistakes of the past, a product of a megalomaniac intoxication of numbers!"

Just as pacifist democratic plans for European federation are unphilosophical, so Fascist plans such as Italy's are not free of the nationalistic-imperialistic aspect of Liberal politics. Fascism may have gone beyond the pacifist sentiment and even destroyed individualism, but it has not yet developed the powers of the personality to take the place of these negative features of statecraft. Jung's own federalistic plans for a European Union are based on the primacy of Germany since the German culture is spiritually the most well developed and geographically the most extensive in the continent. The countries that are conglomerated around the German will be granted autonomy of national culture, though not all countries will be considered equal since not all are spiritually and historically equally developed. The predominance of Germany in Europe will ensure the growth of fresh circles of cultural life that radiate from "the people of the highest achievement".

Alfred Rosenberg (1893-1947)

The political views of Alfred Rosenberg, the most important Nazi ideologue, repeat the basic tenets of German Conservatism (the primacy of the metaphysical personality and the organic nation as opposed to the materialistic and rationalistic individual person or state) and federal foreign policy (the reorganisation of Europe on a basis of autonomous nations developed under the cultural guidance of Germany) with a shift of emphasis from Christian religion to race as the basis of the new world order. In fact, Rosenberg's several writings give the clearest philosophical account of what the new regenerative movement of National Socialism sought to achieve through its doctrine of racial worth and power.

Rosenberg was born in Estonia, one of the Baltic provinces of Russia, and his youth was steeped in studies of the Nordic sagas and the works of Houston Stewart Chamberlain. It was Chamberlain's *Foundations of the nineteenth century* which gave Rosenberg the inspiration to write his own major work *The Myth of the twentieth century* (München, 1930). Rosenberg's philosophical reading included

Schopenauer, Kant, and Indian philosophy, but when he finished his school-leaving examination at seventeen he went to the Technical University at Riga to study architecture. As a student at the University Rosenberg gave a talk in one of the student societies on the Jewish question and later in November 1918, after he had graduated, he addressed a public meeting on the related subject of the Jews and their relation to Bolshevism, a topic which became a major item on the National Socialist agenda.

Soon after this Rosenberg left Russia for Germany. Rosenberg left Russia convinced that the only social and cultural importance that Russia possessed was what the Vikings and the Hanseatic League and immigrants from the West had given it. The Revolution of 1917 meant the defeat of "the formative culture of the Nordic peoples" at the hands of the Mongols aided by "Chinese and peoples of the wastes, Jews, Armenians, and the Kalmuck Tartar, Lenin".[28]

In Munich, which he reached in 1919, Rosenberg met Dietrich Eckart, the anti-Semitic publicist with whom he readily collaborated. Towards the end of 1919, Rosenberg joined the German Workers' Party and when the Party acquired the *Völkische Beobachter* as its official organ, Rosenberg was appointed as assistant to Eckart, who served as chief editor. In 1920, Rosenberg published a collection of his earlier anti-Semitic writings as *Die Spur des Juden im Wandel der Zeiten* which traced the Jewish materialist roots of capitalism as well as of anarchism and Communism. In 1923, Rosenberg replaced the ailing Eckart as chief editor, presumably on Hitler's instructions. When the NSDAP acquired full political power in 1933, Rosenberg was given nominal control of the Party's Foreign Policy Office. In 1934, he was appointed leader of ideological indoctrination and education. Only during the war, in 1941, did Rosenberg obtain a major political post as Minister for the Eastern Occupied Territories, though quickly after assuming office he discovered that he had no real power and that even his subordinates reported directly to Hitler. Rosenberg's personal knowledge of Russia might have helped Hitler if the latter had been sagacious enough to trust his intelligence, for Rosenberg, unlike the other Nazi leaders, realized that Russia could be won only by using "particularist forces against the Muscovite core, overcoming it by means of alliance with the subjugated ethnic groups".[29] At the end of the war, Rosenberg was arrested and tried at Nuremberg,

---

28 cf. *The Myth of the Twentieth Century*, Bk.III, Ch.6.
29 Robert Cecil, *The Myth of the Master Race*, p.19.

where he was condemned to death by hanging on 15 October, 1946.

Rosenberg's political views are based on the primacy of race in historical development. Unlike the other thinkers presented here, Rosenberg did not consider Christianity suitable as a foundation for the new Reich since its various denominations work deleteriously against the interests of the state. On the other hand, the Indo-European world-view, and particularly the Germanic, is based on the racial foundations of honour and fidelity which consolidate the national cultural progress of the European peoples. Opposed to this world-view is the Jewish commercial mentality, which works destructively on the real Faustian conquerors of the world using the stock-exchanges in a supra-national and exploitative way. Indeed, the first World War was the most recent manifestation of the Jewish power of disintegration, as acknowledged by Theodor Herzl, the founder of Zionism, himself.[30] Though, it was the French Revolution which earlier began the systematic destruction of racial worth through its glorification of vulgar democracy and its inauguration of the rule of financial interests through the stock-exchange under the deceptive name of Liberalism. Even the German Socialism of Weitling was falsified into plutocratic communism by the Jews, Marx and Lassalle: "A mass which could have no idea of the worth of the personality let itself be gifted with the "ideal" of a depersonalised world and did not know that this was only a gleaming, empty, phantom".[31]

The destructive work of the Jews who operate from their financial strongholds can be countered only by a racial renewal and a revival of the aristocratic racial heritage of the Indo-Europeans. The new European organisation should not be that of the so-called United States of Europe proposed most notably by the leader of the Paneuropa movement, Count Nikolaus Coudenhove-Kalergi, since it too is democratic and based on the exploitative system of the Jewish international finance, but a hierarchically organised Germanic Empire. As Rosenberg points out, the German Reich has sought during the second World War to enter into

> its old European mission and [to show] in the 20th century that the attitude of the German Reich in the early Middle Ages was no accident but a necessity, a necessity not only because the Germanic-Teutonic power developed itself into fullest elevation, but also

---

30 cf. p.136 below.
31 cf. p.132 below.

because of the knowledge that if Europe wished to preserve its independence, this was to be made possible only through an organizing power on the European continent itself.[32]

The other major European power, France, is clearly under the spell of the Jewish financial rule and bent on destroying the European idea. Only Germany can lead the continent back to life. A precondition of this renaissance is naturally the elimination of the Jews from all the states of Europe. The newly organised Europe will also not continue the old imperialism of England and France but work in a truly federalistic way which grants autonomy to the several national cultures, even those of the East and Africa, which constitute the new world order even while maintaining the leadership therein. This federalism of Rosenberg[33] is of course to be distinguished from the democratic financial federalism of the Jews, just as the nationalism that Rosenberg and the National Socialists advocated is based on a European racial consciousness and strongly to be dissociated from the liberal Jewish championing of nationalism in nineteenth century Europe merely in order to play one nation off against the other for the purpose of their own financial gain. This is why it is possible to reconcile Rosenberg's nationalistic writing with Frantz's denunciation of the principle of nationality and Frantz's and Jung's federalistic views with the foreign political views of Rosenberg and Hitler as being variously significant of the conservative German desire for the rebirth and reorganisation of Europe according to the social and cultural principles of the German people, who have preserved and developed the European spirit to its fullest flower.

*

We see therefore that there is a definite consistency of thought in the most original representatives of German conservatism which considers as the major task of modern Europe the reorganisation of the continent on a truly European spiritual and racial basis which precludes

---

32 cf. p.147 below.
33 cf. in this context, Hitler's attack of the current Jewish fashion of federalism in his *Mein Kampf*, `The mask of federalism'.

the deleterious intervention of the Jewish profiteering mentality and its destructive inventions of capitalism and socialism. The conservative and federalist projects of Lagarde, Frantz and Jung were put into effect for the first time in a major international way by the National Socialists. While the forceful methods employed during the second world war may not have been the best, we cannot any longer fail to perceive the genuine concern to preserve the European tradition which impelled the German rulers of the time. The failure of the Germans in the war has meant a reversion to the very degeneracy that the conservatives were seeking to ward off from the continent in fighting capitalism, socialism and the rule of international finance.

The revival of conservative aims in present-day Europe can be accomplished only by a renewed effort to establish the cultural and social ethos peculiar to the European peoples. To effect this is not at all as impossible as it may seem, though a precondition of its success is a thorough `re-education' of the Europeans focussed on the distinction of their metaphysical tradition as opposed to the stunted materialistic rationalism of the Jews. Even the decline of Christianity as a spiritual bond between the European peoples such as Frantz and Jung envisaged is not entirely a cause for despair, since it is possible to recover the metaphysical sense even in a neo-pagan Europe, as has been brilliantly argued recently by Alain de Benoist in his *Comment peut-on être païen?* (Paris: Albin Michel, 1981).

Only an internal and spiritual reorganisation of the state, however, can help the international organisation of states that must follow. The lead can be taken only by genuine Conservatives such as those of the so-called `new Right',[34] and not by party politicians, whether Conservative or Liberal, who depend on big business and the media for their popularity. It may be noted here that the modern movement for a federalistic Europe called `integral federalism',[35] stemming from the neo-Proudhonian, Alexandre Marc, cannot serve as the basis of the future organisation of Europe since its leaders were Jewish emigrés who settled in France and were concerned primarily to combat the German

---

34 cf. the studies of contemporary neoconservatism by Tomislav Sunic, *Against democracy and equality: the European New Right*, N.Y.: Peter Lang, 1990, and Susanne Mantino, *Die `Neue Rechte' in der `Grauzone' zwischen Rechtsextremismus und Konservatismus*, Frankfurt am Main: Peter Lang, 1992.
35 See Bernard Voyenne, *Histoire de l'idée fédéraliste, III: Les lignées proudhoniennes*, Paris: Presses d'Europe, 1981.

hegemonistic tendencies during the second world war. The federalism of Marc and Raymond Aron can only be another version of Jewish socialism since, in spite of their emphasis on "liberté personnelle", the inherent lack of metaphysical quality and personal freedom in the Jews makes their international enterprise another vehicle for Jewish infiltration of the European ethos. In this respect, 'integral federalism' is only a variant of the Paneuropean movement of Count Nikolaus Coudenhove-Kalergi.

German federalism, as distinct from the French, should be encouraged as far as possible since Germany, in spite of its current liberal democratism, still has a powerful tradition of aristocratic, organic, politics. Hegemonism however should be avoided by Germany, especially in its Greater German form.[36] The leadership of European affairs must rather be shared by the major centres of European culture, Germany, Great Britain, Italy, France, and European Russia. But this can only be done after the national character of all these countries has been refined by a deeper understanding of the spiritual dimension of their respective cultural developments and of the need to preserve this excellence from the debilitating moral corruption, and sterility, of the 'new world order' that is projected by Jewish international finance.

---

36 Austria should eventually be reunited with Germany to form the Central European state proposed by the German federalists.

Chapter I

Paul de Lagarde

Programme for the Conservative Party of Prussia. Sec 9.

Above, the Conservative Party has been determined as that party which is of importance for the maintaining of the strengths present in the nation. It is to be inquired with what means it wishes to achieve this goal.

It wishes to achieve it with those means through which one possesses strength in general, through practice, through food, through rest.

It will therefore see to it that the kingship, nationality, the impulse to industry, art, science, religion, may thrive. It will see to it that the mentioned strengths never lack in supplementation for the materials used by them in work. It will be glad if, for these strengths, after a working day, a period of rest follows in which, through submergence into the unconscious, what has already worked clearly and industriously for a period of time collects itself together and creates the capacity for new work.

The Conservative Party therefore sets forth the freedom of movement, the permission to live a full life, for everything in its programme which it considers as worth maintaining. It rejects the intervention of the state where it is a question of ideal wealth: it rejects this intervention in general so far as is possible, because only the innate strength of the individuals and of the free guilds which wishes to preserve seems valuable to it, since strengths are preserved almost solely through work.

Kingship has been conceived differently in different ages. Now nobody will be easily satisfied with the mystical nonsense of earlier days: all will, if they have also until now presumably not clarified the matter, be agreed on the fact that the king is the steward of the nation. It is incumbent on him, with regard to the entire life of the nation - what in legal contests is incumbent on the arbitrator - to find the common in the diverse and to bring it to validity: it is incumbent on him to serve the future in the present, to precede his people, who must have the confidence that they themselves will come to the point at which their king, who looks farther and therefore chooses the right path, stands before them beckoning. It is a self-contradiction to think of the king as Conservative or Liberal. He is both, or neither of the two, or indeed has actually dismissed, actually thrown the inheritance of his ancestors into the filth. To maintain the kingship of the German sort means to set peace on the throne, means to take up the goad to all disunity of the nation, means to make the contest into a world battle. Such a kingship is conceivable only if the king's personality is informed with the highest and filled to the brim with all the wealth of pure willing, most inquisitive desire for knowledge, unswaying insight, and the responsibility of conscious humility. The king does not have to do, as Hegel, the favorite of the Prussian state, has taught, merely with the peak of formal decision: he is not (like the dean of a faculty) the first, because among many, indeed, one must stand at the top. If a philosopher with Hegel's views is the favorite of a state calling itself conservative, pretending to infallibility, then should the cur still be found which is unpretentious enough to bite such a state. What the poorest and the richest, the most forward living and the one hanging most to the past of his people, feels and cares for should be recognized by the king, placed in its appropriate position, deprived of its negation through the king's friendly Yes, braided into the garland in which violets are not disdained alongside carnations and roses, quaking grass and sedge alongside brome-grass and yew-twig. Woe to the man who ever used the throne for enjoyment: trust that has been frivolously lost is never recovered, and not only would the dynasty fall - every family has to determine for itself what its worth will be - the nation would be a deserted bride on whom the day will never again dawn because dynasties are never elected but always only discovered, the republic however now, after the Germans have taught the world to appreciate its manner of thinking, is the most poetry-less and therefore for men the most unworthy form of political life.

Only that person can maintain the nationality of the Germans - there is no Prussian nation - who perceives that it is as a whole still to be awakened. We obtain this tree only by caring for the straightest shoot that is strongest in the heights striking out again most loftily from the root pulled out from the earth, and fencing in against the wild boar as against the nibbling goats in such a way that God's sun, rain and wind can do their nursing service to it unhindered. We must wait for what will happen: for what is called German has for centuries been the breeding of plant physiologists whose fertilizers and exposure to light influences the plant in this or that way, that is, has distorted it. But in real politics it is never a question of colouring a nationality horribly in lilac or black with the reptile guano scattered on the earth, with Protestantism, with Romanism: it is a question of assuring the nationality that development which the will of God which is to be observed in humility demands. To maintain our developing nationality in growth there are two means to be applied simultaneously: Germany must be set before a task in respect of eternity as well as in respect of the world. It is, as matters lie now, God's grace that Germany as such has no religion, and that it has too narrow borders: for thereby the tasks are shown to it through which it can develop. The battle for a form of piety suited to it inwardly and, secondly, colonization are the means which the still latent nationality of the Germans must rear to a German life.

I have often enough explained that the only way which men can build for the acquisition of a new form of piety is theology.

No power can force any one to take the development of his inner manhood seriously. Force can affect only the determinations emerging into the exterior: it can demand and to a certain degree compel that this and that thing which is to be perceived with the physical eyes happen or not happen, it cannot now or ever demand purity of heart, or indeed demand that it be proven. To strive for purity of heart with success even the environment of the striving person must be purer than our environment is, to flee from which into the country of compulsory schooling, compulsory army service, compulsory inoculation, social formality, breakfast newspapers, of reptilism and similar things is impossible, and in striving against which with not pure hands but those merely reaching out to purity hardly one in hundred thousand succeeds. Force could and should destroy the certifications of the schools, the entire system of instruction in their currently valid form, reptilism, and professionalism: therewith it would purify the air, but not sow any seeds for a future harvest: it does not in general possess such seeds in its reservoirs.

But power can and should say to itself that religion is an even so real and important and interesting object of knowledge as indeed leucite crystals and ascarides, and it can and should say to itself that since it, power, at the moment alone has to determine whether a real existing thing should become successfully an object of scientific research, it is bound to officially recognize religion as such an object and to treat it in accordance with this recognition. If power is so limited as not to comprehend that the existing faculties of the different sorts of theology - because bound in ignorance through obligations to symbolic books or the consideration of the churches and sects to which it has to supply priests and preachers - do not study the history of religion with a free glance for its own sake but nurture advocates for the defence of the residues fallen three hundred and more years ago of a form of piety existing three hundred and more years ago and impossible in our age, then one will have to wait for the moment in which the man of trust of the nation obtains the insight that, as certainly as the national defence system of 1808 could not be in a position to strike the wars of 1864, 1866, 1870, and therefore has been changed by this man of trust personally experienced in these affairs, so certainly do Protestantism and its conscious or indeed unconscious reinterpretations, that is, misrepresentations, exist still only mechanically as burdensome slag-heaps and must be removed: one will have to wait for the moment in which that man of trust will learn that theology is the knowledge of the history of the kingdom of God growing not only in Judaea but from primeval times in all places - for the moment in which that man of trust will understand that the knowledge of the mind may not be called perfectly accessible so long as a knowledge of history of the so-called kingdom of God cannot be acquired in one's fatherland. To this learning of history of the kingdom of God, however, in the measure in which it is taken uncompromisingly seriously, a growth of the kingdom of God itself, at first in the students, and through the illumination of their loving souls, must be attached in all the actions related to them. Where a bridegroom and a bride are at home, love lightens and warms even those who are themselves not bridegroom and bride. There are, when a genius has conquered a new province for mathematics, philology, history, enough hearts to build up the discovered field, and it is not hatred, not the lack of participation, which means building it up: does one really think that it will be different in theology than in the other sciences? Will one love Germany through the study of the German laws and German fairy tales and sagas, but not learn to love the Revelation through the study of the development of Israel, of mysticism, of ritual like those of the liturgies of the Christian Church? Does one think, if one has learnt to love the Revelation from personal acquaintance, that one will not kindle others with this love? Does one think that it is wise to expect advantages for the nation from the learning by rote of a compendium of dogma, of church history, of isagogics[1] if this learning by rote is associated only with the view to a pastor's position, and, as a corollary to that, to reckon that those will harm the nation who, with the certainty of meeting, at first partly the blunt-minded equal validity of those bound through their calling to participation in theology, partly the intentional insults of the most massive sort on the

---

1 Introductory theological study dealing with the literary and external history of the books of the Bible.

part of those obligated through their office to the promotion of everything ideal, will desperately take up martyrdom in the hope of fighting for theology? That theology will not warm far beyond is, to be sure, only too certain: when, however, a shipwrecked person has no more flag to draw attention to himself with, he binds any cloth to a pole and hopes. If we do our duty, the vengeance of God at least reaches the miserable rabble which stands in the way of theology, and the pathetic men who protect that rabble similarly: and that alone is already a blessing.

In the winter of 1849 to 1850 some person[2] worked out a plan for Germany to secure the richly valued south cape of South America as a colonial land: the plan will apparently lie in the trade ministry, in case Mr. von der Heydt thought it worth looking at it and discarding it. At the same time, a German standing in the service of Chile, Major Philippi, turned to the same path without that person knowing of that: his explanation presumably found its grave in the archives of the foreign office. In 1875 that person described, in the *Deutsche Schriften*, I, 84, Austria as the colonial land of the German Reich, and he holds fast to this opinion even today. The minister von Puttkamer[3] narrated in Essen what the national newspaper reported on the morning of 26 October, 1879, and all following mitigations of the press mandarins have not been able to hide the fact that Kaiser Wilhelm publicly made against his will a pact with Austria. Whether concluded unwillingly or willingly (the journey of the Count Otto von Stolberg[4] to Baden-Baden is not forgotten), the pact is there and will remain existing since it has appeared untouchable even to the Count Taaffe.[5] Only when the non-Catholic German-language churches are united under their own rule, when Austria will have acquired so much wit as to strengthen the Siebenburger Saxon and the Zipser German through immigration from Germany, and to direct the German emigration to Bosnia, will there begin to be talk of Austria as the colonial land of the German Reich. In Germany, already for a long time, no reasonable man thinks of letting Austria go: indeed it can become what must be Austro-Germany only if the dynasties of the two states understand the state of affairs: presupposing that the Germans of Austria throw aside the useless Liberal phrases with which they will never achieve anything, even if need

---

2 i.e. Lagarde.

3 Robert von Puttkamer (1828-1900) was a Conservative Prussian who was made Minister of the Interior by Bismarck in 1881.

4 Otto Graf von Stollberg (1837-1896) was Vice-President of the Prussian Ministry and Vice-Chancellor in 1878, as well as Minister of the upper House in 1884.

5 Eduard Graf von Taafe (1833-1895) was a Conservative Austrian statesman who served as Minister of the Interior in 1867, 1870-1 and 1879, and as Minister President, 1879-93.

could perhaps create an advocacy of it: one has however already seen many things become reality which the architects entered into with difficulty and yet are celebrated as the youthful love of the same people. We maintain, therefore, that the German immigration must be conducted quite systematically into the countries of the Austro-Hungarian Crown, whose germanisation has remained stuck or retarded, and we are convinced that, as a consequence of this colonial work, the best aspects of the German character will emerge and benefit the great Germany which extends from the mouth of the Ems to the Roten Turm yoke. The nationality of the Germans does not develop itself now or ever through the Sedan celebrations whose *epitheton ornans*[6] remains held back here out of consideration, and not even through the entertainment which has been performed similar to these Sedan celebrations in Germany either in goodwill or thoughtlessly or through envy of earning money: the muscles of a man are strengthened through work: the muscles of the nation through the work for the nation, and such work is colonisation and in the realm of the world only it is such.

One who now lives of adult age in Prussia and comes from a better situated family has grown up to the belief that Prussia and Russia belong inseparably together. Even the writer of these pages has grown up in this conviction.

In truth, Russia - and in this way was its law to be treated - never supported Prussia, if it did not itself acquire an advantage through the offered help. Russia has been perfidious to Prussia in the most extreme degree, as often as this has appeared useful to it. Which Tsar sat on the throne was a matter of indifference in all cases: for, the politics of an empire is not made by its princes but compelled by the necessities of the actual situation. Every other politics is indeed not worth anything.

The same law which Russia possesses even Prussia possesses, and through Prussia the German Reich, whose Kaiser is the King of Prussia. If at the moment peace is trumpeted, war will come.

Russia counts as a theocracy, as a race and as a burden. It is Catholicism, Judaism and North America taken together. This fact has for a long time not been evaluated sufficiently. The germanisation of Austria alone is in the position of protecting us in the long run against Russia: our 45 millions do not suffice for the defence, that is, in the tension of our Eastern borders. We do not have to deal finely with the Czechs and similar people: they our enemies and must be treated accordingly. They serve the Russians to pluck Austria to pieces which thereafter is to be consumed like an artichoke, leaf by leaf. We cannot hold Austria any other way than by germanising it ruthlessly.

---

6 decorative epithet.

This germanisation is opposed by the Lothringen dynasty which does not seem ever to have heard of the heriditary fraternizations and to believe that a Hohenzollern will hold a contract concluded by it under all circumstances, therefore will not take possession of a Germanised Austria. The Austrian politics is convinced (it is the inheritor of the Roman Empire with its *divide et impera*) that, in its own country, as if it were inhabited by enemies and not by subjects, clever enough to play each person out against the other, and possible to rule through envy and hatred, a constitution cut in the sense of the so-called Conservatives who are found at the moment in possession of power is the highest wisdom, when however such a constitution is a law like all laws, to be changed forthwith, just as another party works at the same high pressure as the one ruling at the moment.

The misfortune of Austria is carefully fostered by the Austrian Jews, who have learnt, as inherited wisdom, to fish in disturbances, and to secure in the conflict of other nations the wealth of all into their own vaults.

The germanisation of Austria is opposed by the Catholic Church which, because Roman, fears Germany even when it is Catholic.

The Catholic Church seeks to expand itself, not only in North America, but indeed very much also in West Asia. On this it keeps silent: that is, it considers what it does there as especially important. It has, apart from the spirit of the times developed from Protestantism, another and indeed a very old enemy, the Greek-Catholic Church.

For a statesman the question will run: Is the Roman Catholic Church or Russia the more dangerous opponent for Germany? Can we besiege Rome more easily through Moscow or Moscow through Rome? The answer is not hard to give. We shall never be free of Moscow if Austria is destroyed, even if we may publish ten times the secret report on that which occurred at the end of October and beginning of November 1850 through the state announcement. It will excite rage enough but rage among us against the Russians is not propulsive enough in the case of equal arming and equal courage of both enemies. Russia has on the east a too open border which it does not need to protect and at which the men are not only born ever anew for its army but can also nourish themselves, whereas we from Germany lose our flesh and blood in distant lands and hunger in Germany. We shall already be free of Rome if we are ourselves, or rather, if we become ourselves.

It would have been advisable to discuss this business with Rome: to be sure, Mr. Falk[7] would then have to be more basically removed than he

---

7 Paul Ludwig Falk (1827-1900) was a Liberal Prussian politician who held the post of Minister of Culture and in 1872 that of Minister of Church, Education and Medical Affairs. Falk was more extremely Liberal than Bismarck and sought to

has until now been removed. To the Mechitarists[8] and all similar orders in Asia, and the Hasunists[9] in European Turkey, a free hand is to be given against the Greek Church and Russia, under the condition that Rome cease to work in Austria and elsewhere at the degermanisation of the Germans. Indeed, Germany shows an interest in Turkey with a good intention, as hopeless as the former is against a Mohammedan power. Armenia is to be established as an independent empire and to hold the field in it open to Romanism and Protestantism, so that war may arise: for war is life, and life and Russia, at the moment, exclude each other for a long time yet. To Rome all nationalities as such are indifferent. Rome, as hostile to Germany as it appears with regard to us, has worked for German culture in Elsace, in Lothringen and Luxemburg, before the German Reich was founded: for, to have differences before oneself is for a politician always more advantageous than to find large flat levels of torpid sameness. Rome is Rome, that means, the Pope is the inheritor of the Imperator: with the Pope as such, who is a political and not an ecclesiastical power, politics may be negotiated, step by step.

The germanisation of Austria is, for Germany, quite apart from what Austria us as a colonial land offers us as help, our internal policy considered from the standpoint of the Foreign Office, a question of life. This germanisation is now harder than it ever would have been before, if the plan sketched in the other volume of the *Deutsche Schriften* had been carried out, harder above all than it was before the Prussian politics discovered the Magyars, a broom which it now would gladly be free of, as once the student of magic of his. It is still possible: it must be possible if the German Reich should remain possible.

This programme was for a long time ready in its basic parts when the reports on Lüderitzland[10] and Cameroon[11] were made known. The sort

---

claim the state's rights from the Church. Falk provoked the antagonism not only of the Catholics in the Kulturkampf but also of the Conservative Evangelical parties who rejected his separation of Church and education.

8 The Mechitarists were Roman Catholic Armenian monks who followed the Armenian priest, Mekhitar Petrosian of Sivas. Driven from Constantinople in 1703, they moved to Venice, from where a dissident group left for Vienna to set up a separate branch (*ca.* 1810).

9 The Hasunists were followers of the Catholic Patriarch, Hasun, whose policy of supporting the Pope and Rome caused a split in the Armenian Catholic Church in 1856. Hasun was subsequently deposed by his more nationalistic opponents though he managed to retain an ecclesiastical position as Cardinal through the mediation of France.

10 Territory in South Africa settled in 1882 by the businessman F. Adolf Lüderitz of Bremen with the support of Bismarck.

11 The Cameroons were annexed along with Togoland by the German explorer Gustav Nachtigal in 1884.

of German colonies that have occurred in South Africa, the settlement prepared in Berlin for the Dutch Boers of the Transvaal, the union concluded in 1879 with Austria, are actually the only joys which the German has had since the founding of the German Reich. Three joys in almost fourteen years: it is little if one considers that souls live quite exclusively on joy.

The principles expressed by the Reich Chancellor with regard to the possession of the German businessmen settled in Africa are to be approved with all one's heart. Everything which lies in the consequence of these principles, as for example the drawing of a post steamship line to be directed to this and that of the lands settled by us will be supported by the Conservative Party as much as it can.

Germany possesses nothing in Africa but, under the protection of Germany, German settlers are possessors there.

Thereby, Germany is exempted from the necessity of sending administrative authorities, and whatever is wont to go along with these, to Africa.

Thereby, Germany has come into the favourable position of letting energetic men produce by their own efforts without their nationality being lost to these men or to their descendants. The light of these characters will already reflect on the motherland. Only, our princes may indeed not imagine that, among their subjects, nothing similar to them lives. The more latent princes there live among a people, the more secure is the monarchy in it: we understand and love only that which we ourselves are or could be. Below people, then, for a long while, nothing, and, above, a Dalai-Lama in uniform - we do not understand the monarchy in this way. The Germans are colonisers, because they cherish a colonial disposition, because the best among them are capable of administering a princely office without much ado: the Celtic love of equality of the French, the Iberian and Semitic self-satisfied racial and familial benightedness of the Spanish, has never colonised and will never colonise: Italy is full in its ruling provinces of Lombardians (Amerigo and Garibaldi bear German names) and for that reason Italy will be able to colonise. Lüderitz, Woermann, Brüning and whatever else they are called, are more princes than the high-titled youth who squander the strength and means belonging to God and their nation with dancers, race-horses and the temple of Moses, and are *à la suite* exiled to some place or the other. Those royal businessmen are thereby exempted in this way, as from many other high princely masquerades, also from the necessity of sinking in love into the arms of colleagues who have, not long before - through the aristocratic Pole Kraszewski – ferreted out the military secrets of their comrades, cousins, and `dear brothers' and friends.

But the Germans who administer their affairs by themselves in

Africa drag along the stock-exchange games of the German capitals, drag along the Prussian school instruction and the press with them. Their children do not need to learn as religion how Abraham, the hero of the faith of the apostle Paul and of the Reformer Luther, slipped the report amongst the Egyptians that his wife was his sister, how the Pharaoh loved the eighty-year-old woman and was punished by Abraham's God as co-agent of the divorce to the advantage of Abraham: they do not need to learn how Isaac imitated this heroic work of his father's in Gerara:[12] learn how Rebecca and Jacob cheated the blind Isaac with savoury roast mutton, and Jehova's promise held fast to this Jacob because the latter possessed it formally, and could therefore stand by his bond - the one who possessed it because he got it by cheating.[13]

Only, it may not be a question in those colonies for a long time of commercial businesses - ostrich feathers and ivory serve only the women of the commercial and commission council - peasants must go back there to the mountains of the hinterlands, peasants who, settling on their own land, build up what they live on with their families. It is possible that then, in case Germany does not come to its senses, even non-peasants may flee there and that they may at some time, with the prospect of the Bay of Whales, lay graves with the inscription: "He has loved the German manner and the law in Germany, and has hated injustice, therefore did he die in Africa".

In both the volumes of his *Deutsche Schriften* the programmer has brought forth proof that the churches of Christian confession are through and through decrepit, that their doctrine, the compromise of the Gospel translated into superstition with philosophies recognised for long as nonsensical, is untenable, their practice unfeasible, their worship without surety and without foundation, even though in Protestantism, understood precisely, there is no ritual. He has deduced therefrom that the state, that is, the institution in which that which is worthy to all and which may not be set up through individuals or groups of individuals is promoted with the means of all, may not come into contact either with Catholicism or with Protestantism or indeed with Judaism, unless it were a question of how these systems were so incorporated so externally and formally into the scope of the implements surrounding the nation in such a way that they stand as little as possible in the way of the members of the nation. If those religious communities have claim of a private legal sort on the state, these claims must self-evidently be satisfied completely: nothing is accomplished outside them. The completion of this, neither Conservative nor Liberal, but realistic, view is, for the Conservative Party, that of caring to see that all those religious communities must be allowed to prove what

---

12 *Genesis* 26: 1-11.
13 *Genesis* 27-28.

they have to set forth against the verdict of science and history which is unfavourable to them, so that they may let their powers develop fully in case these exist without any intervention. Those religious parties maintain that they are powers: well now, they should receive the possibility of hardening their opinion. Healthy human reason, which is not in the position to come in with theoretical recognition or payment of food monies, commands that these communities be left to themselves: not to let them be hindered indeed in the development of their existing capacities is really the task of the Conservative Party. For that reason, the Conservative Party must declare itself, without any reservation with regard to the so-called May Law (only that of 14 May, 1874, has a right to exist) and what has followed it: it must however, as certainly without any reservation, guarantee the freedom of knowledge and freedom to the individuals to give full expression to their religion, insofar as this does not come into opposition, as for example Mormonism does, with the already existing penal-law book, not the one elaborated *ad hoc*. In a wonderful way it is the selflessness through which a self shows itself to be justified: to the religious communities there will remain, in case they wish to be considered as individuals, no other means of setting themselves in power than serving love: such love comes always to the benefit of the whole, and therefore it is a duty of the patriots to maintain it. In that the Conservative Party will strive to let the churches to themselves, in that it removes all hindrances to their effectiveness, it recognizes none of the churches but the sole justified one or the only one justified also as objective, but it recognizes indeed the undying truth that the life of the earth has its gravity beyond the earth. It thereby takes away from the power-holders the possibility of consoling with Heaven the poor people treated here below with *tinctura gummosa*,[14] thereby of idolising, in denial of Heaven, the state, a thing which, quantitatively greater, stands qualitatively on the same level with coffee machines and centrifugal pumps, as the sole legitimate entity, and of depriving the poor of the right of caring for the incidental costs and travel-money for the journey into the bright and yet so unknown land to which the state itself must direct them as much as their conscience bids this care to them.

We have reached now that point of the programme which conceals the key to our position.

Already above it has often been pointed out that the Christian Church knows only one Godhead on earth, the human soul. Here it should be expressed clearly that all activity on earth has, solely, the goal to mature the individual human souls for a higher life, for a life which, however, we shall not deny because we cannot imagine that which we

---

14 gummy dyeing.

should not be able to imagine, so that we may not strive for that whose salvation we strive for for the sake of profit, because we feel it grow from an earthly life pointing to a goal and clearly directed by an instructing hand.

We Conservatives wish to preserve strengths: all other strengths however exist in the human soul or for the sake of the human soul: the souls alone are their own goal. Thus the activity of the Conservative Party is finally summed up in a formula, it wishes to create for every man the right and, insofar as this lies in its hand, the possibility that it really also may become that which God has from the beginning wished that it should become. We are - against the fashionable philosophy of the day - convinced that the world is a whole ordered for a goal, and its disorder is only a means of our education: convinced that every man, simply every man, has a place destined for him, and only him, in it: convinced that all men will be united when every one of them does that, and only that, which he should, since the great music-master seems to have used sevenths and ninths in order to lead into new sorts of melody, and since for that reason - because sevenths and ninths do this - even they must appear in the piece.

It is questionable if, even for the elements of creation - the word element understood in the sense of the chemists -, for the souls, sustenance through work basically matters.

Certainly it does that; only, not in the sense of diary-writing, pietistic, self-tormentors who wish to record evening after evening how wonderfully far they went in the past day, and whose self-complaints are very seldom any thing else but masked self-complacence. The souls do not become something through work in itself, for they do not have the idea of the statue before themselves if they stare constantly only at the marble-block.

They do not become it even through a church, not through a philosophy.

The world goes on secure tracks only because small and large in it stand next to each other, and is there in such a way that the large is not great enough to swallow the small, and the small is large enough to defend itself against the large. Inequality of that which is to be preserved is the precondition of all preservation and all flourishing.

But the will to be oneself of the monads does not order this world; the innate connectedness of the monads which cannot be free of the overruling powers orders it.

All life gravitates in accordance with the central sun: all life lives because it gravitates in accordance with the central sun, and still does not sink into it but circles it.

To teach the existence of God and not to teach at the same time that all created life finds its rest and repose and vital power only in God, is directed only to it, means to deny the existence of God. Man has, in truth, only one duty, that with regard to God from whose Will he has received life and manner of life: the idea of his personality is an idea only insofar as God has thought of it. Therefore, all ethics is divine service, the bondedness to the unique power of the creator of the spirits, of the father of the souls.

The centuries have strained to find the right way to praise this God: if a way was found to do this, the centuries have sung the way till it was sung away and no one wanted to hear it any more. But the centuries have all thought of man as standing next to God, as needing an external means to approach God. But there is no means of seeing God other than of seeking Him in His children.

There is therefore only one divine service on earth, that of serving the children of God: the unborn, the not awakened, the unready, the sick, the lost: those on whose brows the brightness of the heavens shines, and in whose hearts God's blood courses in a perceptibly warm way, just as those timid people living a hard life in whom the light only seldom gleams: those sunk in pleasure and self-interest, and even those most difficult of all to be tolerated, the virtuous, the wise, the correct.

All life on earth is therefore divine service, because everything that exists exists through God, and God is therefore the sole finally valid power of existence: and all divine service is a service to the children of God, whom one loves because one wishes to demonstrate to the Father how much one would like to love Him, if he wished to reveal Himself, and whom one loves because, in their eyes, His eyes gleam, sparkle and love.

All power on earth lies in the children of God, that is, in men. To preserve men as the children of God means to be Conservative in the highest sense.

Therefore, the Conservative Party writes on its standard the education of all living things to the kingdom of God.

With this formula it is said that the education does not have to take place from the standpoints of any particular age, for the kingdom of God does not stand in time but in eternity: that it does not have to take place from the standpoints of any ideality, for ideality is the summary of the ideals of a limited epoch, and even for that reason one-sided, and because one-sided, unsuited to direct souls, which should not be educated as the parents wish, but to that which the children should become: that it does not have to take place from the standpoints of humanity, for man in himself has no worth at all, he has worth only as a child of God: if he is not that then he is an animal, in the best case a fine and loveable animal, which however must show its animal nature as soon as its egoism has been stirred up strongly enough for a reaction.

Those forces whose preservation, one may say, whose preservation alone, matters are the individual souls: they maintain themselves only by serving other souls, each according to its capacity. Diamonds are cut only by diamonds, the children of God educated only by the children of God.

To these forces the Conservative Party wishes to show the goal as also to keep its way free: every step to the goal gives the strength for another step.

Sec 10.

It is impossible, in the programme of a political party, not to take a stance to a problem which holds the whole of Europe, and not least Prussia, in excitement, to the Jewish question.

One who believes that the fate of the human race is directed by God comes as little as the one who is wont to inquire into the natural causes of every phenomenon necessarily into contact with the fact that the Jews are to be found among all cultured peoples, such as are and such as were, that they are hated everywhere to the utmost and at the same time contemned in a wonderful way, and that they are, at least in Europe, the masters of the non-Jews. No one can withdraw any more from the observation that the Jews, to speak with Theodor Mommsen, have promoted everywhere and from the beginning decomposition, that they, as the author of these pages has expressed it once years ago, are the bearers of decay. Even the third fact cannot be contested, that the Jews make up not a religious community but a nation: as such are they considered everywhere, outside the limited circle of certain Berlin notables.

No nation has been so worthless for history in every respect as the Jewish, after the Marian quality in it has fled, as much as completely, to the Church, and the national developed itself further in Islam to a puffball full of the most useless fanaticism, and only Iscariotism on the one hand, and, on the other, the chosen Lord in Israel - childishly conceited about a past whose burnt-up cinders He is, concealing His ugliness with the worn-out fashionable clothes of every previous epoch of Indo-Germanic history and imitating the host in this rubbishy finery - has remained, the decayed noble who has squandered the heritage of his ancestors and now indicates his worth to fools through loud-mouthed behaviour. Nothing, absolutely nothing, of what moves Europe has flowed out of a Jewish heart: the Jews have made no discovery: they have constantly enthused, against the steadily self-developing history, on the side of the immature rebels for a cloud-cuckoo land, and not suffered once for it: everywhere they have hawked surrogates among those who were too lazy to work for the thing that has been falsified by the commercial surrogate.

Only one who is something, and can therefore offer something, is allowed into the life of other nations. The Jew became ethically poorer after 1100 in increasingly quick tempo: he longed allegedly all Sabbath long for the land of his fathers, but did not return to this land, but continued to enjoy himself for six fine week-days at the flesh-pots of the heathens: he flirted with everything which the Indo-Germanic West offered, but he never entered into any marriage with it, in order not to contaminate his blue blood: he learned in this way the grimace of everything which is worthy to us, and, because he can pull this face, he imagines that he has our passion like ourselves and that he stands on par with us. Nothing is serious to the Jew but himself, and the halo of his dark and impenetrable nation. The Jew is everywhere a player, and indeed a bad player, because he remains himself in each and every role: he is a joker, and for that reason often malicious, and every time steadily concerned to maintain the contradictions to play wittily with which is the essence of wit, whereas we wish to balance them in a higher unity: he is a trader, no matter in what, if only it offers either the advantages of wholesale or, like the sale of horses, fashionable goods, antiquities, money and much else, allows to excite the fancy of the purchaser vis-à-vis his own coldness of heart, and in this way to increase the price. The Jew never loves, and for that reason he is never loved.

And because he does not love, because he, so long as he wishes to remain a Jew, cannot give himself up to our ideals, for that reason is he an alien to us, and because he is an alien to us, produces suppuration in our body.

It is doubtlessly not permitted that in any nation another nation may exist: it is doubtlessly commanded to remove those who, even according to the reputed Theodor Mommsen, have from the beginning promoted decomposition: it is the right of every people to remain itself master in its own territory, to live for itself, not for foreigners.

What is called Liberal today will join with what has until now been called Conservative in what has been just maintained, even if the Liberals will presumably be wary of giving public, intentional expression to their agreement with their enemies.

From what has been said it follows that the Jews are a hard misfortune in every European nation. It follows for Germany that the Jews must either emigrate from Germany or become Germans in it. If either the one or the other of these alternatives does not emerge, then Germany will become judaised, to which it is already not just on the way. For, decay strides faster forwards than the growth of life, indeed faster than the growth of a noble life.

How very much Germany has already been judaised is recognized now clearly enough by all who are not seized by the sickness. Would it be possible that we look at the Lazzis of Jewish wit, that we enjoy Berthold Auerbach's through-and-through ungerman and consciously unchristian stories,[15] that so many of us, indeed bureaucrats, play at the stock-exchange, that our nobility has served as factotum for the swindle of our foundations, if we were not already interpenetrated with Palestine? How could a Prussian minister appoint to a German university a man like Mr. Graetz,[16] whom not only Mr. von Treitschke, but even a basically racially proud Jew, the popular philosopher Moritz Lazarus[17] - celebrated not long ago in an incredible manner in the *Vossische Zeitung* of 14 September 1884 - has characterised in Zarncke's literary *Centralblatt* of January 1872, how could the people overlook the atavism and the impotence of those who do not wish to give up their poisonous hatred against Christianity, to whose light too they convert, and which alone protects them from being removed by force, how could something like that happen if the German did not lie in a fever?

Now, the *Torah*, 5, 9, has, in a chapter of naturally often doubtful logic, expressed that Israel has not maintained the so-called Promised Land by virtue of its own righteousness and honesty, for Israel is a stubborn people: it received that land first on account of the crime of the previous possessor, secondly because Jehova promised it to them. The latter reason does not hold, not in general and especially not with respect to Germany, which Jehova has never glorified to the Jews. So there remains the former. One who lets it be valid must also let it be valid that those who receive a land on account of the crime of the inhabitants lose the legal claim to this land only when that crime ceases.

If we insert instead of the word `crime' used by de Wette the appropriate word for Germans, `sin': Luther translates into German in a genuinely Protestant manner "godless nature".

There is for man only one sin, that of not being himself: for by the fact that he is not this he rejects the one who has willed his existence, and wished it as such and such a definite existence - not the one born of flesh and blood but the reborn - the existence become ethical, the sacrament as which every man should wander through the world unites spirit and body inseparably, and, because he is a man only in this inseparability, awaiting the resurrection of the body after death.

What is true of man is true also of nations.

---

15 Auerbach (1812-1882) was a Jewish novelist noted for his tales of village life, *Schwarzwälder Dorfgeschichten*, and other similar rustic novels.

16 Heinrich Graetz (1817-1891) was the author of a major history of the Jews. He was appointed to the faculty of Breslau University in 1869.

17 Moritz Lazarus (1824-1903) was a Jewish philosopher and psychologist, founder of comparative psychology.

We must break with humanity: for our most personal duty is not that which is common to all men, but only that which is proper to us is. Humanity is our sin, individuality our mission.

Only through individuality shall we defend ourselves even from the Jews. The more sharply we form our character as a nation and the characters of all the individuals tolerable in our midst, the less place there remains in Germany for the Jews.

We want, for that reason, a strong monarchy which, if it takes care of itself, and wishes to maintain itself as much as possible in Germany, will not flirt with the Synagogue: we also want the risk of recognizing unpleasant aspects in it, an aristocracy, to be sure, not such a one as advises its sons to marry Jewesses or indeed such as promises in the Berlin newspapers three thousand thalers to the one who helps to gild a countly crown become unrespectable with a million from the stock-exchange profiteering: we want churches as energetically as these can become anywhere without the help of the state, and do not at all fear their anathema, since life, just as they have only just been placed quite on their own strength, may lead soon to the insight that the sun removes the cloak of the wanderer sooner with its warmth than the wind with its blowing: we want persons, as many as vital persons as possible, none of them like the other, even if they should occasionally conflict with one another. We reject the jelly of 'humanity' as an inedible one and the spirit of the century of the same, which is however only the spirit of the Liberal newspapers, therefore the demon of the Pincus Honigmann, who has not become historic, and of the comrades of this Honigmann. We want as much as little a state because the man himself should exist, help himself, and not cry for the policeman and the great purse of the taxpayer, and for that purpose however may also demand to receive his manoeuvring capacity freely. Germany should become full of German men and the German manner, so much of itself as an egg: then is there no room for Palestine in it.

Thus that which matters in the Jewish question is linked in the most intimate manner with precisely that which the Conservative party has recognized as its task: to maintain its strengths.

The Jews are, as their prophets have often said to them, a stubborn people. They possess will. But the Gospel seeks redemption not in the will but in the breaking of the will, in the cross, which is a foolishness to the Jews and an annoyance to the heathens. If every nation of Europe crosses the will of the Jews, the Jews will be redeemed from themselves, and thereby, and only thereby, we from the Jews.

Already now it is clear that all Jews who come into contact with the serious life of the Indo-Germans, are subject to it. Until now, no Jew who has studied Greek philosophy, German history, German music with his heart, has remained a Jew, and none of those so alienated from Judaism may maintain that all really German hearts did not beat cheerfully and constantly warmly next to his: even then did they beat against his when he, like another Cordelia, did not speak the word demanded by a new Lear, to be sure, to his external death. Jewish boys develop themselves in a German school in case a German teacher fond of them stands in front of them, and the class is attended by German children of some talent and some sunny nature, at all times free of Judaism, which wins the upper hand in them once again only when they return as job-seekers into the circle of their nation or, in riper years, are repulsed by Germans alienated from them. Mixed marriages provide German descendants as long as the German part of the marriage is more than an average Prussian product and the Jewish is devoted to some not specifically Jewish life-content, such German descendants that the unthinking do not at all think that they see before them in these mixed marriages not pure German children.

Not every Jew is talented enough to come into an intimate relationship with Indo-Germanic science and art: and many who would be talented enough for it do not come into contact with it at all. But every Jew comes into contact with individual Germans. If we are so illustriously honest, so full of warm love, so calm-minded, so upward breathing to the great homeland above as we can be, if we wear our hearts on our sleeves - it would not be good if, under the dumb rock buried under which the Jewish soul groans, it, not free from itself, did not feel us and it did not become ours. It is the fortune of good men that they build around themselves through their existence a temple in which the bluntest becomes prayerful and the hardest tender. Do you really think that, if Germany were full of such men, Israel too would not pray to, not its Adonai, who is an idol to us, but to our God?

Germany is now indeed the heart of Europe. If the Conservatives of Prussia can resolve the task of destroying Judaism in the mentioned way, then it is resolved for Europe. And it must be resolved, otherwise Europe will become a field of death.

In the measure in which we become ourselves will the Jews cease to be Jews. But we can then become ourselves only if the Prussian educational system with its gregariousness - this terrible monstrosity, not system, which only courts the unchristian Christianity all the time because it is heathen but seeks from cowardice to assume the local colours in a world illumined by the Gospel - will be eradicated from the root, only if we will have established, in the place of freedom, equality and fraternity, the three other principles: the right to become what God gave us to become, inequality which alone makes possible a polyphonic movement, and the quality of being a child of God.

Because the Conservative Party follows these principles, it indeed is called to make an end of the Jews. To take in the Jews into the present Prussia of Altenstein[19] and Falk means to make Prussia Palestine: to take them into our Prussia means to remove them through their rebirth. And they must be removed.

---

18 Karl Freiherr vom Stein zum Altenstein (1770-1840) was a Prussian statesman and Hegelian thinker who sought to subject the Church to the omnipotence of the state. His political career included terms as Finance Minister (1808) and Director of the Ministry for Culture, Education and Medical Affairs (1817)

Chapter II

Constantin Frantz

Federalism, Chapter XVI: Untenability of the principle of nationality.

Whatever great technical difficulties may also stand against the foundation of a central European federation, on which we do not deceive ourselves in the least - they would be able to be overcome indeed step by step with the necessary circumspection, energy, and persistence. The chief difficulty lies much more in the disposition of the minds, in the limited views and false ideas which still rule us upto the present. So, to start with, the idea of the state, with which in any case nothing can be achieved where it is a question of a task extending far beyond the state, and on which we have already earlier expressed ourselves sufficiently. Further, however, was bound with the idea of the state the principle of nationality, which, if recognized, would make the foundation of a central European federation, which would clearly exclude nationalistic tendencies, in general impossible.

1.

If therefore this principle faces us as the most powerful hindrance, we shall have to combat it so much more because it first confused minds properly in that it awakened passions. However the state remains in a certain sense an abstract being, of whose matters and interests the great masses understand only little, and wherewith everywhere only a comparably smaller part of the population occupies itself seriously. The principle of nationality, on the other hand, works as if with the energy of a natural principle, for everyone feels himself as a member of a nation, and moreover it requires indeed no special knowledge or considerations, already language does everything here. If now the people are still persuaded by talk that even making their nationality valid is their most important and holy matter, they are then sufficiently light-headed to become fanatic that they fall upon one another like beasts.

Indeed, really like beasts, in that the proclamation of the principle of nationality includes in itself to a certain degree a letter of abandonment of reason and equates men to animals. For, finally the matter runs to the point that one acts as if the different nationalities existing at the moment were as much firmly established types given from nature as the different species of animals. Germans, for example, and Frenchmen, or in general, Teutons and Celts, would then like to behave with regard to one other as dogs and cats, between which there exists an instinctive antipathy, and similarly is it with other nationalities. Peace would be possible under such presuppositions only if every nationality had its special field, and at best closed with a Chinese Wall where secure natural boundaries did not already exist.

What however is so indisputably certain than that such national types given once and for all are a pure chimera, since the nationalities themselves arose rather first in history. And they did not arise indeed merely through the fact that a family in the course of the generations grew into a people but - the Jews, at most, excluded thereby - under continual mixture with foreign elements. If this is proved for the present-day Romance peoples already by their mixed language, it is also not very different with the Germans speaking a so-called original language - at least considered physiologically. The ancient Teutons were not autochthonous in Germany, and they did not find the country entirely empty also any longer during their immigration. There lived there already men of Finnish-Uralic race who however were doubtless subjugated, from whom indeed partly the subject peoples who existed among the ancient Teutons may have arisen, and who however thereafter gradually merged with the free peoples into one, whereby thus the Teutonic blood was mixed with foreign blood. But if that may be considered as a mere surmise, it stands firm however that south-eastern Germany contains Celtic elements, as certainly in still greater measure north-eastern Germany Slavic elements. Quite untenable therefore is it to consider the present-day Germans as an original people who crawled out from the earth, as it were, or fell from the heavens.

No, what the present-day Germans are, that they have become only in the course of history, in the main not very differently from what has happened with all nations. And just as now the nationalities change according to their inner being in the course of history, so also do their territorial boundaries also change. Physically weak or intellectually less developed nationalities withdraw before stronger or more highly developed, and can be gradually fully absorbed by the predominant nationality, even without powerful suppression. The proofs of that are found as far back as historical documents reach and hardly anything different is to be expected than that in the future too it will happen similarly.

If therefore the nationalities are themselves only historical structures, and seized according to their inner being as well as according to their external expansion in continual change, in no way can an absolute significance be ascribed to them too, they can have only a relative worth. And that we recognize also fully. For although themselves only historical structures, they are however, as such, the most lasting in comparison to others. States can fall completely in which the nationality of their population continues to live still for a long time and possibly indeed pushes forth new blooms. If, now, in general the present always rests on the residue of the historical past, nationality also contains to a certain degree the spiritual essence of this historical residue. To that then is attached the feeling and thought of the racial comrades, and receives therefrom a certain complexion and direction. Incontestable also that the national consciousness gives a certain attitude to the peoples and is itself, on that account, not without a certain ethical worth. Above all, people feel themselves to be free when they act according to their nationality, into which they were born, so that their own inner being is merged with it. Therefore, nationality does not work like an external law of compulsion but even as an instinctive one, according to which they seem to follow therein only their own inner impulses. Only, that is not in any way true spiritual freedom, it can be caught, in certain circumstances, in the greatest prejudices, but it is natural freedom, which the people do not wish to have harmed. Hence, the resentment and the resistance which every disregard of nationality and open attempts at subjugation naturally call forth.

And in this way now is explained the present-day forced emergence of the principle of nationality as a reaction against the absolutism of the previous century which almost fully ignored the nationalities and often inconsiderately slighted them in that it treated the peoples only as a taxable and recruitable mass. They were estimated as a mere material for the state according to the number of people, according to their usefulness for strategic and commercial goals, just as indeed happened even at the

Vienna Congress.[19] The suppressed or wilfully torn apart nationalities felt this inclemency, they demanded thereafter their natural right to be treated according to their nationality which they wished to see expressly recognized. But just as every reaction shoots beyond its true goal, the validation of the nationality became then became a goal in itself. Precisely as if the peoples had nothing more important to do but to conserve and develop their nationality and the sole guarantee of their welfare, as well as, at the same time, the symbol of the true, the good and the beautiful, lay therein.

From such a standpoint, to be sure, all other considerations had to be silenced before the demands of the nationality. Further, in order to bask properly in this way in the glow of their nationality, the peoples had also above all to strive thereafter to see it decorated with laurels, and to produce as large a domain for it as possible. But when that had become a universal principle - what could indeed follow from that in practice but that every nation, as soon as it felt itself strong enough and the opportunity for it offered itself, fell upon their neighbours in order to tear a part of their territory from them, for only such undertakings and successes guaranteed them the proper enjoyment of their nationality. And for that reason did one war follow another, for which the pretext was found increasingly more easily. It is clear therefrom how the principle of nationality contradicted itself through such consequences, since what the rights of every nationality should have allegedly protected would finally end rather with the negation of all international law.

2.

If the nationalities are only historical structures which rise and fall in history, they may not wish to be considered as something holy or divine. Only in the heathen world could such a significance be ascribed to them, because the heathen gods of the peoples themselves were considered as individual special beings who therefore also could have a special relation to the individual nationalities. The true God as such even remained concealed to the heathen peoples, and therefore did they not succeed in recognizing one another. Then indeed when the divine belief attached to

---

19 International assembly of monarchs and diplomats between September 1814 and June 1815 to reestablish the political order of Europe after the Wars of Liberation against Napoléon. The former Holy Roman Empire of the German Nation was at this Congress replaced by a loose confederation of the German states.

their nationality lent their national life a special glow, there arose however precisely therefrom the Roman world-rule finally absorbing all nationalities, through which the principle of nationality was actually conducted *ad absurdam*.

What then lies basically assumed in the present-day nationality-enthusiasm if not a return to heathendom? The roots of this confusion reach back even to the age of the Renaissance where the minds were filled with antique ideas, which indeed emerged at first only as scholarly and aesthetic dilettantisms, later however penetrated also into the political thought and finally made itself valid also practically. In the great French Revolution indeed one referred back openly in many respects to ancient Roman models, and if there should be tribunes and consuls once again, why not also a cult of the state, of which admittedly a beginning was also made. Progressing in this direction, did in his time a Kossuth[20] prattle about a special Magyar god, of the God of Arpad, whom he appealed to for help. And what else did the motto of Mazzini,[21] *Iddio e popolo* bespeak? Even the same does it signify when the nationalities are represented in the form of female divinities, whether it be as statues or in imprints on coins. Either that is, in general, senseless, or it should really aim at an apotheosis of the nationality. Thus now we have also received a Germania, and, in addition, a Borussia[22] and a Bavaria. And there were indeed added to the provincial goddesses city-goddesses as well so that we got to see, at the celebratory entry of the troops in Berlin in '71, also an Argentorata, a Metzia, and a Berolina. One could to a certain degree think of an ancient Roman triumphal procession. And such a heathen misconduct in the Reich "of fear of God and holy customs"! Does one not seem to think at all that those female statues recalled to a certain extent the goddess of Reason whom one once led around the streets of Paris? This here incidentally.

What is, further, so clear than that, in the Christian world-view, the nationalities are in no way to be considered as created by God and graced

---

20 Lajos Kossuth (1802-1894), the Hungarian leader of the revolution of 1848-9. Kossuth was an extreme nationalist and opposed to Hungary's subordination to Vienna. During the revolution, Kossuth became virtually dictator of Hungary but with the intervention of the Russian armies, he had to flee from Hungary to Turkey and England.

21 Giuseppe Mazzini (1805-1872), the Genoese revolutionary who founded the secret society, Young Italy (1832) and championed the Risorgimento movement which sought to establish Italian unity. Mazzini was an uncompromising Republican and led the short-lived Roman Republic which was proclaimed in 1849 but brought down by the intervention of the French army at the request of the Pope.

22 Prussia.

with special gifts, so that thereby one was preferred above the other by God. Rather, the nationality is not worth anything in general before God. If it pleased Him to make the small Jewish tribe the vessel of his Revelation, this happened even only as a preparation for the Christian Revelation offered to all peoples equally. For God has created only man as such and therewith mankind. But after mankind scattered itself and split into individual peoples, it is not indeed God's will that now the peoples should pursue their special national glory, but that they gradually feel themselves one again, as a herd under one shepherd, - that according to the Christian doctrine is the divinely willed goal! For that reason the Christian peoples should consider themselves and act even as Christians, that is commanded to them by their religion, that they, on the contrary, feel themselves to be Germans, as Frenchmen, etc., is a merely historically founded relationship which then makes itself afterwards valid as a natural instinct which is also to be regarded as such but to clothe which with a religious solemnity is to be considered as decidedly unchristian. It is also quite inappropriate for the Church if it, on its part, wished to participate in it, instead of which it should first of all educate its believers into good Christians and thereafter to uprightness, not however encourage the nationality-craze.

If we read in *Genesis*, that God created man in his image, there must indeed lie in the human essence a reflection of the divinity, but not in the nationality, which belongs merely to this world, and therewith is something merely earthly and transitory. Or does one think indeed that we would still figure also in heaven as Germans, Frenchmen, etc? Quite certainly, as little as there will be still Kaisers and kings, ministers and generals, or tailors and cobblers there. All that disappears into nothing as soon as we leave this world. But if only human souls are immortal, not nationalities, how indeed should we conduct a cult of nationality?

So little does something absolute lie in the nationality that rather in those accomplishments of men which in comparison are most undying, that is, in the works of art and science, at the same time even the national peculiarity recedes most. Science strives merely for universal validity of its knowledge and insofar as it would however like through this striving to be influenced more or less by national feelings, that is nothing else but a defect unfortunately not to be removed entirely, because even the scientist cannot spring out of his skin. Birth, education, and environment influence his way of thought, he can never defend himself entirely from them, least of all in the field of intellectual sciences and indeed in historical research, insofar as national history comes thereby into play. If now it is indeed founded in the essence of art that it cannot entirely lack a national stamp, because the artist has to consider at the same time the receptivity of his public, still the incontestable fact lies before one that precisely in the greatest art-works the specifically national once again withdraws most, and therefore also the great artists are only those whose works find an understanding in the entire educated world and can seize the minds of men. The essential in their works must therefore indeed not be that which finds itself to be national therein but the universally human, and therewith the supra-national.

This is valid then for the more recent arts which developed on the ground of Christianity even more than for the ancient arts. If, accordingly, in the Greek tragedy there is expressed at the same time the spiritual substance of Greek culture, one can certainly much less say that through Shakespeare the Englishman speaks. For many of his most excellent works (among which *Hamlet*, as his masterpiece) treat in general of no English national material. If, however, Goethe's *Faust* is related to a specifically German tale, it is rather the greatness that the poet introduces us therewith into a circle of ideas encompassing humans, demons, and God, through which this wonderful poem forms to a certain degree a counterpart to Dante's *Divine Comedy*, which finds its admirers in the entire Christian world. And what is true now with regard to poetry is confirmed also in the plastic arts. Let us observe, for example, Dürer's famed Apostle. Something German is not to be denied therein, but that does not form also its worth, but it is the apostolic spirit which looks out of the German faces. What indeed would have to be said of architecture? There lay indeed in the Gothic so little of something specifically national that it once was expanded over the entire territory of the Western Christianity, but the national thereby called forth so few peculiarities that one could hardly compare it to the different dialects of one and the same language. Whether in Scandinavia or in Andalusia - the basic character of the Gothic architecture is the same and betrays itself at first glance. If however, towards the decline of the Middle Ages, the Gothic was driven out by the Renaissance, tell me still in which country indeed since then has a specifically national architecture emerged? It happened nowhere. Furthermore, precisely since the principle of nationality was proclaimed expressly, architecture has become so much more characterless, so that it seeks itself today in all styles without being able in any way to attain to a new firm type.

So helpless does the principle of nationality show itself here to call forth higher spiritual creations! If now we already saw how it leads itself in the political field *ad absurdam*, it has become in our present-day architecture an irony of itself. As, for example, when one built in Berlin a so-called national museum, in general as a building which could stand as well in Naples or in Petersburg. And what picture will indeed the future

German Parliament building present? Who knows whether it will not also perhaps appear in the Greek style, most presumably however it should have presented itself as a Renaissance building with a quadriga and diverse pictures of gods on it, whereby however it may be opined to us nevertheless that one sees therein a creation out of the original spirit of the German nation. For this indeed stands firm today: we must be in all things German national, for what reason do we live otherwise under the regime of National Liberalism? The German spirit must have arisen there by force.

No, I say, it has fallen, that everyone must acknowledge who compares the present-day tone-setting representatives of German intellectual development with the men whom we possessed earlier. They to be sure spoke little of their Germanness, and they did not in general wish to be specifically German, but for that reason they were really great minds. Today the great mouth which hovers over the German culture apparently causes that it rushes like water waves therein, only, no spirit hovers over the waters, it seems to have drowned therein. If it should emerge again, supra-national universal ideals will be required for it to raise it up.

3.

Those are the two basic errors with regard to the principle of nationality: that one wishes to consider, on the one hand, the nationalities as given natural types or, on the other hand, as divine creations, instead of which they are in reality purely historical formations. This character they share thoroughly with the state. The essential difference however thereby is that, if the nationalities arise from themselves as it were, and develop themselves in the manner of a natural growth, on the contrary, for the foundation and further development of the states the human activity, the consciously intentional must also come in because the state is in all circumstances a community of aims, therefore it has for the achievement of its goals special organs. For nationality there are no goals, but how it is, because it is, without consciousness of why it is, thus there arises from it also only an instinctive pressing towards this or that, from which indeed results may arise but not deeds, whose ground is rather the state, or the Reich, and the federation. For that reason national life and state life are nowhere identical, even where the two seem to coincide externally. The entire history of the states proves how the states nowhere emerged from mere nationality, but everywhere were and are human institutions or foundations, whereas nationality has only the character of an actual condition. If now the state is a community of aims, for that reason is even everything which somehow forms a community of great importance for the state, and therefore above all also nationality, in that it forms through language, as through a certain equality of feeling, of thought and aspiration, an instinctive community which precedes the conscious community of aims, so that without any national foundation however once again no state development would be possible. But because, in the foundation of the state, freedom has its role, and intention predominates, the state development is bound to quite different conditions than the national development. For that reason, on the ground of one and the same nation, indeed, many different states can arises, just as, on the other hand, one and the same state may encompass different nationalities or fragments of the same.

That this has happened always is once again proved by the entire political history and if with regard to it there emerges the demand that state and nationality must coincide, then there lies at the basis of that even the erroneous identification of political and national life. If there really existed such an identity, then the chief striving of the state must be to bring its nationality to fruition. The state however should rather strive for the good and therewith indeed foster the good characteristics of the given nationality, and try its best, on the other hand, to break from the bad characteristics, which are not lacking anywhere. If these two things happen, then the nationality too will develop itself thereby so much more excellently that is then effected as a consequence, and in no way should the excellence of the nationality itself be considered as a goal for the state, rather, that is the heathen cult of nationality.

If, further, the state is at the same time the organ of universal human development, it would in no way correspond to it if the states limited themselves everywhere nationally. For, thereby the different nationalities become only so much more obstinate with regard to one another, lodge themselves in their peculiarities, and in this way the progress of civilisation would be restricted by the lack of reciprocal stimulation. From this standpoint it therefore appears as a true blessing that in any case the great states encompass everywhere different elements and that there are, alongside the states with dominant national foundations, also states with dominant difference of components, like Belgium, Switzerland, and, in great style, the Austrian monarchy. Similarly, even the United States of North America form certainly no real national body. And why indeed should not different nationalities be bound to a whole, if thereby their political goals are better satisfied than through reciprocal separation? That then should be judged according to the predominant circumstances, but to discard such unions from the start would be a purely wilful opinion. Only, even the constitution of such nationally collected states must have a federative character so that a sphere of independent development remains to the different nationalities.

If the nations are, in reality, nowhere autochthonous, but have attained to their areas of settlement, where they finally establish themselves only under the co-operation of many events, partly still lying in darkness, and if the nationality-boundaries have then later been displaced many times, relations have then often arisen as a result of this which would make a political demarcation according to nationality quite unfeasible. One would have to attempt to politically undo once again the artificial work, for example, in the Baltic provinces, to separate the German, Slavic, Finnish, and Lithuanian elements. In this way, even in Bohemia, the Germans cannot be separated from the Czechs, much less the half a dozen different nationalities which live close beside one another in Hungary. To make the principle of nationality valid there would mean to conjure up a chaos. But as regards the question of rights - how should one hold the mere principle of nationality against such conditions that have arisen from the course of history, since the nationalities themselves however are nothing else but historical formations, and have no other legal claim to show than that they are even there?

To recognize this is what is most important here. If, on the other hand, one considers the nationalities as structures existing in and for themselves - no matter whether they may have crept out from the earth or fallen from the heavens - then the axe would be laid to the entire historical political structure. Everything must be broken up and placed on new foundations. The principle of nationality would then work even as destructively as if one wished to bring all of a sudden differences of wealth - resting no less everywhere on actual processes and therewith pertaining to history - into a new order. But if one thinks that the one as well as the other has been attained - what would that mean then but that from then on all freedom of development should cease? For, just as individual freedom leads inevitably to inequalities of wealth, so the free development of the states and nations to political and national inequalities. Some rise, others fall and are under circumstances quite absorbed. This battle for existence - to use but a favourite phrase of our times - is simply not to be removed from the world, or there should in general be no history, which however forms the actual realm of the entire human development.

4.

Least of all does the forced desire to make the nationality principle valid agree with the real conditions of development of our age, as they emerge most strikingly in the field of public communication. If the principle of nationality lead logically to the demand that the different nations, in order to develop so much more according to their particular quality, would have to seclude themselves as much as possible from one another, they rather actually come increasingly closer to one another through the enormous upsurge of all means of communication. They are acquainted with one another reciprocally through personal communication, through trade their material interests are entwined, through the press the ideas circulate as never before. And is it not precisely such an upsurge as it has become for a long time a commonplace to glorify as the highest triumph of our age? Indeed, is one not concerned most eagerly to promote the international communication so much more through telegraph-, post-, trade- and currency contracts, and does there not emerge at the same time also increasingly an international private law? What is it then but that one would like to raise with one hand nationality-walls which with the other hand one continually tears down? Strange contradiction!

Precisely for Germany is that most valid. For, as the European central country it would be least suited to seclude itself into a national body, instead of which it must feel itself permitted through the present-day course of things so much more to return to the universal idea of the Holy Roman Empire. It is clear then that we, as the conditions exist now, are directed most to a narrower binding with our eastern neighbouring countries. Not only because the German culture has grown up inseparably with the Slavic, but as, on the one hand, from thence threaten the greatest dangers for our future, so, on the other hand, would a correct politics open to us also the greatest prospects therein. If nevertheless we feared indeed to contaminate our nationality through a closer communication with the Slavs - oh, then we should never have crossed the Elbe and Saale, or accepted Bohemia into the German Reich federation. It is good for us that our forefathers thought differently in this respect, otherwise Germany would today actually extend only to the Elbe, the Saale, and the Bohemian forest. And what indeed would such a narrowly restricted Germany signify, no matter how concerned also we may be to develop our nationality, in order to be able to bask then in the idea of the special excellence of the same! The other nations would recognize such German excellence so much the less, the more they themselves, for their own part, however move into nationality-tendencies.

If the matters of the entire Western Christianity concentrated themselves in the former Reich - according to its idea - and if our forefathers had the lofty sense of grasping this idea, then it would reveal in no way any new upsurge of the German spirit if today already the idea of a central European federation appeared to us as extravagant. And was it not precisely in that age, when the old Reich, which was called expressly not German but Roman, existed still in power, when nevertheless the German nation developed itself really individually, in its public institutions and laws as in its customs and life-forms? On the other hand, what is today, when we have allegedly attained to a purely German national Reich - I say, what is in the constitution of this Reich really originally German alongside all other institutions and laws of the same? Certainly very little. Then again, in the present-day public expressions of our intellectual life? Just as our theatres continue to perform translations or imitations of French plays, so our entire entertainment literature is imitated more or less from foreign models, according to which even our newspaper system receives its style, especially as regards the famous institute of a semi-official press, except that there the reptile base can indeed be considered as a novelty. If we glance first at the external forms of society, including clothing, decoration of homes, etc, what is supposed to be considered fine is there almost thoroughly French, in the object as well as in its name, upto the kitchen, whose actual accomplishments are signalled by the `menu'. Much different however was it with our forefathers. They behaved as Christian Germans, and without making much talk of their Germanness, they really gave their life a national stamp which one has to seek with a lantern in the modern Germany flooded with gossip about nationality.

Fine Germanness, say I finally, as whose loudest spokesmen and most active social leaders we see today rather the Jews emerging, who apparently understand best what belongs to a German Reich, what German law, German customs, German style and elegance is. Now indeed they understand masterfully to exploit the entire nationality humbug to their advantage. And in order that we may not like at all to observe how we are led by the nose and exploited by these intruders, who have settled among us parasitically, there must, to be sure, be so much more talk made of German national spirit and German national greatness.

Indeed, does it not already emerge in the whole of Europe that in the same measure as the nationality tendencies made themselves valid, as a consequence of which it however lay that every nation had to reject all foreign influences, rather one nation after the other fell to the constantly growing influence of the Jewish people entirely foreign to them in blood, spirit and way of thought? That would then be the end-result of the nationality tendencies, that the Christian peoples afterwards would become merely the train-bearers of the Jewry, to sink to which the modern Germany is already fully in the way. But that even, I think, throws first the full light on the untenability of the principle of nationality. If we therefore are thereby permitted to view this threatening Jewish rule closer so we shall thereby at the same time attain to a recognition of the true task of our age.

Chapter XVII: Incidental Observations on the Jewish question.

Already for the sake of the final goal of our entire work we cannot avoid taking even the Jewish question into consideration, as certainly as the present Jewish rule itself belongs to the greatest hindrances to a federative development. But, in general, the insufficiency of the political science until now has emerged nowhere so strikingly and in such disastrous consequences as in the maxims derived from this science for the treatment of the Jewish question. From our standpoint we shall reach quite contradictory views on this point and must therefore be prepared for it from the start for that reason to be labelled with the title of a mediaeval unenlightened person and fanatical devourer of Jews. That would do nothing to us, however, for we indulge not in mere opinions but support ourselves on actual pieces of evidence and on arguments derived from the nature of things against which already there will be nothing to raise, apart from the fact that one had to try to contradict them, which meanwhile remained to be expected. Now the pieces of evidence and the arguments themselves.

1.

If the political thought had not for a long time now fallen into the confusion of starting from abstract general concepts, instead of starting from the observation of the real conditions, nobody would close his eyes to the fact that the Jews form not only in the religious field but also in state and society a quite special element. Most strikingly in the manner of their material existence, in that they everywhere do not live so much on the products of their own labour but rather attempt to exploit the labour of the remaining population. To be sure, they are not inactive, but their significance lies not in productive but in lucrative business. Only where their number is too great in relation to the remaining population for them to nourish themselves entirely through trade activity do they, out of necessity, take up also other businesses, to which however they know to give at the same time a commercial direction as far as it is indeed possible.

Especially, coarse strenuous manual labour is almost entirely avoided by them. Agriculture they conduct only very exceptionally, but if they acquire great agricultural property, then it happens almost always in the intention of an advantageous resale, or in any case for a lease, or if they actually worked the same, it would happen with Christian workers. Jews seem to be too good for farm slaves. Even for factory workers, but where the Jew invests in a factory, apart from the accountants, indeed only the factory managers and supersivors are Jews. Thus even the Jew who has become well-to-do has Christian servants, a Christian coachman drives the rich Jew, exactly as if it were Christians who built the coach for him and even more his house. Christians who manufactured his clothes, his furniture and all the luxury items with which he surrounds his existence. Christians who produced the means of nourishment for him, indeed who also plastered and turned the streets along which he struts and drives, as finally also Christian guards and night-watchman once again care for the safety of his precious person and his property.

Now I ask, if, in view of this thing lying before the eyes of every man, it can still be somehow said that the Jews show themselves entirely in the same way as popular and state comrades as the Christians do? And how can one indeed demand civic equality in the case of such a great inequality in the actual life-conditions? Is the foundation on which the existence of all states and nations rests not the material work for the production of food, clothing, housing and domestic equipment, and how much of the work required for that do the Jews then undertake in relation to their numbers? Certainly not the hundredth part, whereas they are represented in all businesses that are more lucrative than productive perhaps a hundred times more strongly than the Christian population. Certainly, if in our official statistics for every professional class, even the religion of the concerned individuals were cited, so that one could see from it in terms of numbers what work the Christians and what the Jews undertake, one would be surprised at the disproportion.

But one may perhaps say: that does not concern the state: what business its citizens take up and from what they wish to feed themselves, that must remain left to every person insofar as he thereby acts according to the law; even the free choice of profession belongs itself to the most primary civic rights and so it does not redound to the blame of the Jews that they withdraw from material work if they know how to feed themselves better in another way. And that is indeed perfectly right: in terms of the law there is indeed nothing to be complained about against it, after the Jews have become fully franchised citizen; but so much more is there to be said: that such a people which in the same measure in which it avoids material work, on the other hand seeks to draw to itself all lucrative businesses, may not in general be accepted to equal civic rights.

It is senseless to speak here of humanity and tolerance, whatever that nonetheless may have offered! Thus, offered that the Christian population had to take up coarse work so much more than was necessary to satisfy the concerned needs for the Jewish population. Or, expressed precisely: that the Christians had to labour for the Jewish masters, so that the latter could live so much more comfortably and be set so much more in a situation to devote themselves to businesses which run to the point where they at the same time bring to themselves as much as possible even from the remaining work-products of the Christian population and can fatten themselves in such a way through the sweat of the Christians. Oh, if the Jewish masters had to use their hands to produce food, clothing, housing and domestic equipment, and if they wished to be served, and for that could accept only people of their own race, then even only a relatively so much smaller part of them would be able to turn to trade businesses or indeed to the scholarly professions than the Christian population. Only then could there be any talk of equality of rights and duties. Instead of this, however, matters lie in such a way that the Christian population, as thanks for the fact that they accepted these Semitic foreigners into their country, are exploited by them, and decline in the same measure as the latter rise.

But even if, of the Christian population, a part does not conduct any manual labour but feeds itself through more lucrative businesses, and in general lives somehow in a more preferred position, the same civic right is still very reconcilable with it. For, the higher strata of the Christian population remain nevertheless through the bond of blood always bound to the great masses, they cannot become a closed caste within which all wealth is concentrated. On the other hand, the Jews form in the same measure in which they are in relation to the Christian population only a tiny minority, so much more also a body holding together fast within itself, which is indeed a closed caste since they marry, with rare exceptions, only among themselves. And it will always be so, equal civic rights, and even civil marriage, will not basically change anything. It follows therefrom that the wealth acquired once by Jews also remains always within the circle of the same. And since now - because they conduct almost only lucrative businesses - their wealth increases yearly, therewith increases also the disproportion between the wealth of the Jewish and of the Christian population. Soon it must come to the point that the greatest part of all moveable property would find itself in the hands of the small Jewish minority. And one may well consider how mortgages also especially belong to moveable property, whereby landed property is mortgaged to them, how, according to the situation, through the state papers found in their possession, even the entire state as such is mortgaged to them.

Who does not see in this way how a state and social question of the first order lies before one. A question which is ramified so broadly into all social and state relations that, without taking this very thing into account, every thorough reform would in general become impossible.

2.

One may speak as much as one wishes of humanity and enlightenment, which the equalisation of the Jewish population with the Christian offers, but there always remains the fact which cannot be denied, and which lies before the eyes of the whole world, that the Jewish people has been proved to be an entirely exceptional existence through its own history and is proved even to this day. For, that the Jews, already in the Middle Ages, so long as they formed a more or less independent communal system, appeared as a singularity is proved by the common judgement of all those peoples with whom they once entered in contact. When however the last remainder of their national communal existence was destroyed, it was not less unparalleled that they dispersed themselves since that time through all countries. And thereupon, however, that they, without example, in spite of such a dispersal, held fast to the peculiarity of their life, in that they never merged themselves in the course of so many centuries with the surrounding medium.

If the Jews may nevertheless accept the language of the peoples among whom they have settled, and to a certain degree even the external life customs, that cannot indeed be otherwise than if they wish to exist in the medium surrounding them, where they form for themselves nowhere a compact mass, nor even produce themselves their own food requirements; in the core of their being, however, they remain unchanged. For that reason there are indeed German or Polish Jews, etc., but not indeed Jewish Germans or Jewish Poles, etc., but to speak in this way would mean to reverse the facts, because the principal element in the German or Polish Jews is indeed Judaism, and on the other hand, their Germanness or Polishness only the covering that has appeared later and, as it were, clothed the Jewish core. As Jews, however, they must so much more be considered as a special element as they themselves consider themselves thus.

Or, wherein consists the nature of a man if not in the consciousness which he has of himself? But now nothing is more certain and well-known than that the Jews consider themselves as the chosen people, and that this is not indeed an opinion merely accidentally accepted by them, which they could possibly - as one thinks, through the progress of enlightenment - leave behind. But precisely this belief is the constitutive factor of their life, through which they first became a particular nation, and through which they were distinguished especially also from the remaining Semites, so closely related to them, hardly less than from the Japhetic tribes. It was merely the revelation become part of their patriarchal heritage, and then further developed through Moses and the prophets, as a special pact which Jehovah made with them to which their national character was related and on which they rest to this day. Only if they gave up these beliefs in their chosenness would they cease to be a special nationality, and from there on be able to merge with other nationalities just as indeed Slavs or Frenchmen make themselves German. But that is indeed the point, that, among the Jews, nationality and religion are inseparably one so that they would have to first give up their religion in order to be able to lay aside their nationality and become indeed real Germans.

It is entirely nonsensical therefore that the Jews have been considered only as a special religious society wherein then there lay no hindrance that they nevertheless may become perfectly German, whereas, however, they consider themselves even according to their religion as the chosen and, consequently, a quite special people which has so little in common with the German culture as with any other nationality. Precisely more senseless is it to wish thereby to cite the example of the different Christian confessions as if the Jews, alongside Catholics and Protestants, formed nothing more than another confession. Just as the Catholic or Evangelical confession - thus does one argue further - does not do damage to the entire German nationality, nor to the civic and political equality, why then should the Jewish confession do so? Oh, if Judaism were only a special confession, then there would be in Mohammedanism, in Buddhism, and in Fetishism also only special confessions. I say however, a shame for the country of thinkers that it gossiped of a Jewish confession, and let the demand of equality of the Jews with the Christian confession be loosely talked about! Even - incidentally noted - a sad proof of how it must be ordered in the case of religious instruction in our high schools, where indeed the people educate themselves who later rule and make the laws and lead the public opinion, but thereby do not seem to know at all any more what confession really means and what, on other hand, religion.

Now then, what religion really means emerges most pragmatically in the Jewish religion which, according to its own explanation, consists in the pact which Jehovah has concluded with the patriarchs, and has thereby made the descendants of the same his chosen people. And is not Christianity once again called expressly the New Covenant, through which that Old Covenant was extinguished insofar as, through the Christian revelation, an equal relationship to God was revealed to the whole of mankind. That however the Jews disavowed, but, supporting themselves on the old book become decayed, they still wished to be held continuously by their God as His darling, around whose fate the entire world-history had to turn. But it turns for eighteen centuries rather around Christianity, instead of which the Jews, as a result of their stubbornness, were dispersed throughout the world and, as the eternal Jew, or pass through the world as, as the French language so pregnantly says, the *Juif errant*: damned as a people to be able neither to live nor to die, to a certain extent living mummies, and as such, at the same time, living proofs of the revelation. For, truly, it required nothing but this so entirely exceptional fate of the Jewish people, so thoroughly contradicting everything that was otherwise naturally to be expected, to reach the conviction with regard to them that here powers had to be in effect which reach far beyond humanity, enlightenment and reason, and in which therefore nothing can be changed with all such talk.

However - let us continue - far from the Jews being brought to their senses through the fate thrust upon them since the destruction of Jerusalem, and leaving their stubbornness, they only fell into so much greater hard-heartedness. Since that time, like Shylock his document, they have tapped their Old Covenant, and because their national glory had in the meantime become rather contemptible, they believed so much more to be able to hope and claim that Jehovah would some day produce and have to produce a so much more brilliant revenge. From the idea of the chosen people, therefore, the monstrous consequences were drawn in the Talmud which briefly ran to the effect that all other peoples were pledged to serve the Jews and to work for the Jews, who in turn were not pledged to them for anything. In addition, there are bound with such views expressions of the most raging hatred and the deepest contempt of Christianity as, much more, of its originator. And even this Talmud has won authoritative validity among the Jews, it actually exercises a greater influence on the Jewish way of thought than the entire Old Testament.[23]

---

23 [cf. the excellent writing of Rohling, *Der Talmudjude*, based on a study of

Once again, therefore: where does equality remain here, if the Jews however, according to their religious belief, do not consider themselves in any way as standing on par with the Christian population, but consider themselves as elevated far above it? But where indeed remains equality if, on the one hand, the Christian youth are directed to considering the Jewish religion as a divine foundation and the Old Testament with reverence, whereas, on the other hand, the Jewish youth through their religious instruction, to put it most mildly, are filled with contempt with regard to Christianity and especially with regard to its originator, as with regard to the entire New Testament? Thereby it is well understood if even this cannot be at all otherwise so long as the Jews remain Jews, wherewith indeed also it is immediately given that they repudiate Christianity basically. It must be a miracle, if the consequence should not spring from that that the Jew views the Christian with quite different eyes than, on the other hand, the Christian the Jew.

And, with regard to him, one wishes still to speak of equality, which then must come to be recognized especially also in the civic and constitutional position! Truly, if such a view should be the fruit of our progressive enlightenment, then the apostolic statement is literally valid:

"Dicentes se esse sapientes, stulti facti sunt".[24]

3.

Quite nonsensical further, if one maintains now or wishes to hope, that even the civic and political equality would lead to the Jews laying aside their special nature. Even if they may really assimilate themselves in their external appearance and attitude more to the Christian population, and even if the so-called enlightened Jews may desist from many external principles of their religion so that, for example, they eat also pork without repulsion - how little indeed does that change the core of their nature? For, so long as they remain, in general, Jews, they can also never cease to consider themselves the chosen people, and therein lies finally the practically decisive thing. For, what then will the civic rights which are lent to them serve them but that they offer them the means to bring so

---

basic sources, already published many times and which everyone should have read who wishes to participate in any way in the Jewish question.]

N.B. All footnotes provided in the original sources themselves are inserted in brackets.

24 *Romans* I:22, "Professing themselves to be wise, they become foolish".

much more effectively to practical exercice the claims to exploitation and mastery stemming from that belief? More effectively, besides, for the reason that the external assimilation of the Jews with the Christian population going along with it distracts at the same time from their business, since the rich and educated Jew now enters into society as a gentleman, like others, and the more freely he moves in all circles upto the highest the better, also, he can go about his lucrative speculations.

If the first beginnings of the present-day Jewish emancipation reach back - very clearly! - to the age of the Enlightenment, then one may consider however whether the Jews, as thanks for the freer position guaranteed to them, have gradually since then begun also indeed to take up a greater part of the material work, to conduct agriculture and handicrafts, or to become indeed stone-cutters and wood-cutters? That would be something. They sought only so much the more to bring the lucrative businesses to themselves, to play a role in society and to obtain influence on the public affairs. That proceeded then gradually until 1848, when they suddenly demanded equality. What an upsurge the Jewry since then underwent every one knows whose own experience reaches back to beyond 1848. But the Jewry underwent a new and still greater upsurge since 1866 and, finally, with the founding of the new German Reich, from when on the equality proclaimed in 1848 first achieved full actual validity, and, through the universal freedom of movement a so much greater field of speculation was opened to the Jews. And they have then exploited that with an energy and, if one wishes, with a fatefulness which could demand our wonderment, if the destruction of the German nation in body and soul were not implied thereby.

Not only the stock-exchange and the press fell, with few exceptions, to their mastery, or at least under their influence, but also the entire economic legislation that emerged since that time; as also nothing else was to be expected when, indeed, there stood at the top of the tone-setting parliamentary party a Lasker.[25] And have they not known to make as good a business of the *Culturkampf* as with millions? Since that time, in all fields of life, the Jewish influence accosts us, often as decisive. How will

---

25 [Nevertheless a remarkable little person, only, to be sure, the most remarkable in his case was that this basically so limited and superficial head could play such a role. For if the poverty of his mind were not already visible in his parliamentary activities, they emerged so much more clearly through his lucubrations "on the world- and political wisdom", with which he wished at the same time to shine as a writer, thereby displaying the most vulgar material, and furthermore in a repulsive Jewish German.] Eduard Lasker (1829-1884) was a parliamentarian and founder of the National Liberal Party (1866).

it be after a generation! For, since the wealth of the Jews increases in geometric proportion, so, in the same measure, even all businesses demanding capital will go over into the hands of the Jews, especially the entire commerce. And what may be still more important: even the public offices, the entry to which is conditioned by a costly preparatory education, because the average much higher standard of living of the Jews gives them also so much more the means to let their sons be educated for the state service, as, in general, for all those professions which similarly require a costly preparation. And what can the consequence of this be but that, then, in the judicial and administrative bodies, as in the medical personnel and the technical personnel, finally the Jewry gains the predominance? Indeed, why not also in the personnel of the higher educational institutions, as soon as the same will have once fully divested themselves of their earlier relations to the Christian Church, as is already demanded for the elementary schools. That truly would be a fine condition if the Jewry not only rules the stock-exchange, trade and the press, but also imposes the means of influence on everything which guarantees public positions! As one said in Germany at the beginning of the 16th century, when almost half of all the landed property had fallen indirectly or indirectly into the possession of the Church:

What kind of system is it?

We cannot recover from the priests.

so will one then have much more to say:

What kind of system is it?

We cannot recover from the Jews.

Or is that not to be said already today?

There live in Germany relatively more than ten times as many Jews as in England and in the Romance countries, so naturally even the Jewish question is for us of much greater practical significance than there, and the consequences of Jewish emancipation disturbing the entire popular life must therefore also emerge so much more quickly and strikingly among us. No matter what role the Jewry has played for a long time even in France, where even the emancipation emerged earliest! What influence the Jewish bankers exercised under Louis Philippe and exercise upto the present day is known to all, indeed it seems very much that the Jew Gambetta may become in the near future the leader of the French Republic. He already begins to anticipate this position.

But, in general, - how the Jewish influence has risen in the whole of Europe since the French Revolution! Already the financial rule of the big Jewish bankers, in which to a certain degree the entire modern Jewry finds its most peculiar representatives, is considered as almost the normal condition. All governments pay homage to this financial rule as to a legitimate power. And should the Jews not foster still higher ideas from the legitimacy of this power of theirs? No doubt that they will glimpse therein nothing more than even the literal fulfilment of the promise once made to the Jewish people which we read in 5 *Moses* 15:6:

> Fenerabis gentibus multis et ipse a nullo accipies mutuum,
> dominaberis nationibus plurimis et tui nemo dominabitur.[26]

If this promise, however, actually comes into fulfilment, it happens merely as a consequence of the lack of understanding and the carelessness of the Christian nations. It is high time that they finally pull themselves up and begin to consider the facts in their true light, but not through the glasses which they have had put on them by the Jewry itself.

4.

If the disastrous step of the Jewish emancipation has once been taken, then the Jews can now freely drum for their constitutional rights just as they beat on the old covenant which Jehovah once concluded with their patriarchs, and on the basis of these constitutional rights nothing stands in their way to their drawing to themselves all the instruments of power and thereby to preparing quite unnoticed their actual formal mastery. One cannot encounter this today effectively at all apart from the fact that the civic equality must be fully revoked.

That this indeed would have the hateful appearance of a law of exception cannot be changed after unreason has brought it about that what must be considered as, in and for itself, self-explanatory seems, in retrospect, rather to first require a special justification. For, what is in and for itself so clear as that a being which forms a singularity actually not only everywhere but even considers itself to be that should, for that reason, also be treated as a singularity? One could not in general speak of exception in this case because however every exception presupposes rather more the rule and that means here equality presupposed as its *prius*, whereas, on the other hand, the singular is therewith also the one unequal to everything else. But in this way there lay also the *proton pseudos*[27] precisely in the fact that one wished to bring the essentially unequal under

---

26 *Deuteronomy* 15:6, "Thou shalt lend unto many nations, but thou shalt not borrow; and thou shalt reign over many nations, but they shall not reign over thee".
27 the first falsehood.

the same law, whereupon one is, to be sure, necessitated to remove once again through exceptional laws the equality decreed with so little deliberation.

In order to become fully clear on this, let one ask only: in which shape did the Jews come to us originally? Certainly, indeed as foreigners and, according to this, it depended merely on the discretion of the state authorities under what conditions they wished to let in these foreigners in general. They could claim only human rights unconditionally, much different however is it with the civic and political rights leading beyond that. All that could have been granted to them in this respect was special concessions, which had nothing in and for themselves to do with the provincial constitution and with the general provincial law, but then formed a special Jewish decree to which also special control regulations corresponded. The Jews had thereby not in the least become state citizens, but they became state comrades who, as such, stood under special laws. It should have stayed at that for always, for that was the sole principally right treatment of the matter, as, on the other hand, even the Jews themselves could not raise any legal claims to anything more.

If one wished to object to this, indeed, that they could have acquired the state civic rights through usucaption, even this would be quite untenable. For, even if they might have lived in the country for so many centuries, what does that change when they nevertheless always remained a singularity which just did not suit the general law? But, for that, the Jews themselves would have had to be emancipated from their madness of being the chosen people, as - what goes along with that - from their hatred of Christianity, and, on the other hand, from their avoidance of material labour; then the conditions would have been different. But if they have not done the least for such self-emancipation, and if one nevertheless accepted them into the general law, that was merely an act of irresponsible rashness of legislation, similar (only thousand times worse) to what is present in the permission of freedom of usury and of the general entitlement to draw bills of exchange, both of which may also be related to a certain degree to the Jewish emancipation itself, and is today already recognized and lamented on many sides as an error. Now - as laws are made, they can, in retrospect, also be changed once again or, in general, removed. Good God! how often have in our own age already entire constitutions disappeared without a trace after a short existence, and why indeed should the civic rights of the Jews be considered as untouchable, which however is of the most recent date, whereas already so many old dynasties have lost their rights of rule? But, as regards the form of the exceptional laws which eventually have to be issued with regard to the Jews, thereby only the same thing would occur first of all which will have to happen with regard to the general capacity to draw bills of exchange, after one foolishly enough had explained the right to draw bills of exchange - which by its nature is appropriate only for commercial circles, and otherwise seems permissible only for individual special categories of persons - as valid for the entire population, and then, to be sure, would be able to reach a tolerable situation only through an exceptional law whereby one excludes fully numerous classes from the right to draw bills of exchange. Further - have not for years exceptional laws been issued against priests and recently against the Socialists? And truly, exceptional laws against the spread of the Jewry would arouse the least odium in the country. Apart from the Jews themselves, no noteworthy part of the population would grumble about it, or indeed present actual difficulties for that purpose to the state authority. On the contrary, addresses of agreement and thanks would prevail only in this way.

I say further: the state authority must consider itself obliged indeed to protect its wards from the Jewish exploitative system which disturbs the entire economy so much the more since it arouses everywhere at the same time the instinct of wishing to enrich oneself through speculative undertakings instead of through productive work, when one sees, indeed, how good it turned out for the Jewry. A moral plague has arisen out of this which the state administration is first of all obliged to ward off. And if it itself still believes in Christianity - would it not be obliged by the same to protect the Christian population from being distracted from their faith through the uninterrupted effect of the Jewish press, and misled to unbelief?

Truly, one who ponders these matters more deeply must indeed glimpse precisely its most serious side. For, the Jewish mind can even not work any other way than through dechristianisation, as certainly as Christianity is and must be to the Jew an object of his repudiation, so long as he remains a Jew. That he may indeed; in his own religion, however, he should not, for that reason, be offended. But that does not give him the right to found a press which works uninterruptedly at the burying of Christianity, while, on the other side, the state would have much occasion to take the consequences arising therefrom into consideration because therewith, at the same time, even its own existence is buried. For, it stands firm that the entire state structure of the new Europe dates from the spread of Christianity, and has its most important moral support in the Christian faith, so that if the latter were destroyed, following it even everything else must collapse quite automatically. How incomparably much less, on the other hand, do the Socialist attacks against property signify? And if the Socialists thereby proclaimed atheism at the same time, this itself - even on account of its open emergence - is much less dangerous than the uninterrupted but mostly indirectly and half-hiddenly conducted attacks against Christianity, wherein the entire Jewish press and Jewish literature is active. Who now is the dangerous enemy: who runs his head against the wall, or who undermines its bases like a mole? In addition, - how incomparably much greater means of help there stand at the command of the Jewish agitation than to the Socialists, against which one nevertheless thought it necessary to intervene in such a draconic manner, while the Jewish press may continue its business undisturbed and the entire Jewry still has the advantage thereby that, through the Socialist-noise, the public attention was so much more distracted from their activities.

Even quite generally considered, the intellectual influence of the Jewry cannot work other than destructively. For, in the entire development of modern Europe, which is indeed inseparably interwoven with Christianity, the Jewry has sneaked in, as it were, or parasitically penetrated. Even not organically grown along with it, but finding itself in the impossibility of ever feeling itself at one with it inwardly, a true development from inside can also nowhere be considered, but insofar as the Jewish mind nevertheless grasps at the development, it comes as if from outside and it remains an external affair. In addition, the Jews have also nowhere appeared creative in a higher sense, we owe them not a single great discovery or invention, perhaps only the invention of the drawing of bills of exchange excepted, not a single real new life-stimulating idea.[28] Their most peculiar talent is rather to exploit the ideas worked out already by others, in that they bring the same into a new *façon* and therewith mould them into current coinage. Their effort is above all directed to effect, therefore much less is it a matter of inner truth with them. The facts speak for themselves.

---

28 [Even Spinoza (to whom one is wont to point as to the founder of the entire modern philosophy, and who indeed was for a time celebrated even by Christian thinkers so excessively, which however it has already ceased to do) possessed in no way the spirit of initiative. For, quite apart from what he may have got from the Kabbala, he received however much more the impulse to his entire philosophising first from Descartes, from whom really the entire rationalist philosophy dates, and who, at the same time, has, through his mathematical and physical discoveries, to which Spinoza for his part has nothing to present, acquired for himself an imperishable name in the entire history of science. Therefore the Jews should not so exaggeratedly magnify their Spinoza, especially since they had cast precisely this man, whose intellectual significance should remain uncontested on our part, even from their midst. But, as regards their Moses Mendelssohn, who is considered by them as the second great thinker, one reads today in every history of modern philosophy that he was nothing further than a Wolfian appearing in tasteful form, and therewith a zero for the development of philosophical knowledge.]

What has opera come to through Meyerbeer,[29] and what has become of it through an Offenbach![30] Similarly even Heine[31] has, in spite of the flashes of genius which cannot be denied him, in retrospect only harmed German poetry and literature. What indeed would have to be said of an Auerbach,[32] to whom besides Heine's gifted nature is lacking? If Immermann[33] has created in his *Oberhof,* based on the peasantry, a work of original vitality, on the other hand the village stories became for Auerbach a lucrative industry. In a word: thus does it stand today that the intellectual influence of the Jewry, with the help of the newspaper press, ruins the German literature and German language just as much as the Jewish speculators ruin the national economy with the help of the stock-exchange.

If the mission of the Jewish people were concluded with the appearance of Christianity, so that it continued to vegetate in the development proceeding from then on just as a history-less people itself, it has, to be sure, for that reason - because not inwardly participating in this development at all – become so much the better able to consider, cold to the heart, what in a given case might have the most chances for itself, and accordingly then to adopt its own attitude. On this rests the influence which the Jews have known to acquire in the general politics, or more precisely expressed: the skill with which they have known to exploit the process of events to their advantage. What successes were to be achieved there, since the entire European state system began to break apart at its hinges with the French Revolution, and, with the wars arising from it, the system of state loans received previously unthought of dimensions! If, at the same time, the earlier natural economy was transformed into the

---

29 Giacomo Meyerbeer (born Jakob Meyer Beer) (1791-1864) was a German Jewish composer who achieved success in Paris with his grand operas.

30 [cf. in this context, Richard Wagner, *Das Judenthum in der Musik,* along with the devastating critique of the Meyerbeerian nonsense in *Oper und Drama.*] Jacques Offenbach (born Jakob Offenbach) (1819-1880) was a German Jewish composer of operettas in Paris.

31 Heinrich Heine (1797-1856) was a Jewish poet famous for his volumes of poems, *Das Buch der Lieder* (1827), *Neue Gedichte* (1831) and *Romancero* (1844). Heine moved to Paris in 1831 and wrote a series of newspaper articles about the new democratic order in France as well as the revolutionary heritage in Germany (i.e. the Reformation, the Enlightenment, and the modern critical philosophy).

32 See p.38n. above.

33 Karl Leberecht Immermann (1796-1840) was a German dramatist and novelist. His *Oberhof* formed part of his novel *Münchhausen* (1838-39) and presented a realistic study of village life and tradition.

money economy so that now, for the private economy as well as for the state economy, the money system became the most decisive factor, for the handling of which the Jewish mind is naturally disposed, the Jewish bank system had to develop so much more quickly into a world power in that the entire Jewry, in spite of its dispersal through the Christian countries, exists in a continuous connection. A connection which has indeed acquired through the *Alliance israélite* even already a formal organ, wherewith then the Jewish world-rule thus already begins to constitute itself.

And in view of this, should the state authorities - instead of taking up energetic measures against the spread of the Jewish influence as long as there is still time - calmly lay their hands in their lap, letting the matters proceed unhindered until the noose is thrown around their necks? No, here if anywhere would laws of exception - which, as shown sufficiently, would rather signify the return to the natural situation - not only be allowed according to emergency law, but be considered as simply demanded.

5.

If, finally, we consider the Jewish question further from the federative standpoint, the judgement is, through what has been written above, already almost given. For, as certain as the Jews consider themselves to be the chosen people, which stands high above all other peoples, just as they also actually represent everywhere an entire exceptional element, so certainly are they from the start to be considered as an essentially anti-federative element within the Christian world. For that reason the federalist is doubly obliged to enter against their activity, to fraternize with judaising tendencies would mean for him to make a breach in his own system, because a federative political and social development would therewith become impossible.

And no less impossible a federative ordering of the relationships of the nations - in relation to which the anti-federative character of the Jewry naturally first properly emerges, since the ideal of the chosen people does not indeed aim at a free union of peoples but at ruling all other peoples in the future. In this respect, would not the ancient Roman maxim, `divide et impera' have occurred to them, whereas it is obvious, however, that the unity of the Christian peoples would at any rate turn a Jewish world-rule into an empty dream for ever? Or should the means be lacking to the Jews for the `divide', after they have won already such a many-sided influence on high politics? On the contrary, but also in this respect precisely the so-called emancipation offers them only so much more effective means. For, first of all, they have since then so much better opportunity to explore the reciprocal relations of the different states for the large banking houses, for which every important notice is as good as ready money. Less apparent is it how the Jews, as soon as they were once recognized comrades of the people, entered immediately also as the most chosen leaders of opinion of every nationality - playing among us the genuine German patriot, in Hungary the full-blooded Magyar from the time of Arpad onwards, in France the enraged Frenchman, etc. - and in this way contribute now not less their phrases of nationalism, in addition, in order to arouse the nationalities against one another. From this follow always new wars - pure profit for the Jewry, in that the great stock-exchange princes who maintain themselves most conveniently out of the line of fire then provide the loans required for the wars. The dissension of the Christian peoples and the desolate finances of the states become for them true gold mines. And should not therefore the Jewry be considered a powerful hindrance to the international federation, since rather the opposite of it is for them a true question of existence?

If however, therewith, the practitioners of the so-called gold international, as well as the danger of the same, appear for the first time in full light, it is also clear how the individual states in their isolation in general do not possess already sufficient means of protection against it. But there is no more help against it apart from through international organisation. And so we see ourselves led through the Jewish question to a new and still greater problem.

Chapter XVIII: The international organisation.

If we stand now before the last and highest stage of federative development, the most difficult task is also therewith presented. And difficult not only on account of its compass, as on account of the many and great hindrances which are thereby to be overcome in practice, but also on account of the newness of the matter, for the proper understanding of which the general consciousness has been prepared only a little.

Not indeed that it is in general not spoken of, or will not be spoken of, but, as a thing to be wished for, the international organisation perhaps already appears to everybody after some deliberation. Only, there lies the difficulty that this idea has not yet amalgamated itself with the general political thought in such a way that it represents itself as a necessary consequence of the otherwise recognized principles, but as something incidental, which therefore one can also entirely ignore. Precisely in the manner in which it occurs in the upto now ruling political science, from which indeed, on the one hand, the general thought receives its direction as, on the other hand, it itself only reflects the general state of minds.

And now it is an incontestable fact that this science concentrates on questions of state organisation, wherewith openly no regulation can indeed be given for the questions of the organisation of the nations. But then, the relationships of the nations are observed at most according to their legal aspect, which however does not extend far for the organisation, and the international law is considered once again as something entirely special, which has nothing in common with private law and political law, or indeed perhaps could remain out of consideration for a political system. In this way, for example, does even the celebrated Stahl[34] proceed, for whose so pretentiously treading and still so deficient wisdom the world relations seem indeed not to exist at all. It is clear, therefore, how the demand of an international organisation, according to its theoretical aspect, includes at the same time the demand of a scientific revolution in itself which is also beginning to be actually realized.[35]

Quite correspondingly therefore to that limited conception of the matter on the side of the ruling science are the international questions at the moment still considered as an external matter which has nothing to do with the questions of internal development. Federalism (as we already know) is, from the start, beyond such a division of internal and external politics, but, if the division is granted, then the external matters form the special domain of diplomacy which is concerned with all its powers to conceal its activity in the veil of secrecy. And there one still speaks of public life! Oh, it is indeed worth the effort to debate heatedly in the parliament on this or that state position, often on a pure trifle, whereas diplomacy can contrive wars in absolute silence which cost the people, in

---

34 cf. p.94n. below.

35 [The first impulse to this was given by the Frenchman, Auguste Comte through his 'Sociology' – Indeed, a bastard expression, like 'bureacracy', which however has already become gradually naturalized, and which should designate here the systematic treatment of all the questions related to the human communal life. Once this idea has been comprehended, it is obvious that in any case the state is only a special form of the human community, and consequently sociology has, from the beginning, a far wider scope than the so-called political science of today and that then especially also the observation of the community of nations belongs most essentially to its tasks. In this way, in Comte, it is precisely also the international organisation in which his entire world-view is concentrated. We shall later, from another point of view, return again to this man.]

retrospect, billions. If then nothing helps, they must eat the soup which the high politics has brewed for them and thereby, in addition, put in their own bones besides. Does not the thickest absolutism lie therein, whatever else still ought to be called so?

In the case of such blinding on the real significance of the matter, it requires, to be sure, no further explanation for the fact that the question of international organisation does not, in general, stand in the catalogue of major questions, whereas however - as a consequence of the emergence of the Socialists - it has already at least come to the point that today the whole world speaks of the social question and hardly any one any more challenges the existence of this question. But how then, - does the international question perhaps not exist? Good God, is the existence of this question not proved by the ever-growing military burdens under whose pressure the people are bowed? And how should one ever, under such a state of affairs, think of a thorough social reform where all state relations stand as on a powder-keg? Where the governments are occupied - instead of with the organisation of work - with military organisation, where the military budget absorbs all material aids of the state, and where it already seems as if the invention of new attack- and defence-weapons are to be considered as the highest triumph of the human mind.

But whence is this sad situation? It is even as little a product of natural necessity, to which one had to abandon oneself involuntarily, as the present rule of capital and the entire social decay which arose rather from human self-interest, as well as from the negligence, carelessness, and thoughtlessness of public authorities, who let things happen as they may, or take up only ineffective and failed measures against them. And precisely in this way arose militarism from the self-interest, indolence and thoughtlessness of the peoples, or from their power-holders, and just as there the means of remedy are to be sought in social organisation, so, here, in international organisation.

Indeed it lay now before the noses of the Socialists that, without a lasting system of peace, no social organisation is to be hoped for. And they have, for that reason, actually taken the international organisation into consideration. But, indeed, - how? For, if even their own social projects show themselves to be essentially unfeasible and untenable, their international projects require in general no serious criticism. There is lacking there in those people from the start the possibility of a right understanding of the task, which is indeed not to be approached with merely economic concepts, wherein, however, the thought of the Socialists is concentrated. Rather, one must proceed there mostly from historical considerations, as certainly as the peoples and states are in and for themselves even historical structures. What they have become today and how they conduct themselves today with one another is then similarly conditioned through the historical process and, in consideration of this, arises consequently the following question: what possibilities and what impulses of development are therewith given and how far can one work in a regulating manner? But that goes far beyond national economic questions. For, if indeed also the material interests form a bond for the community of nations, the far more decisive factor lies in the moral and intellectual field and only religion can give the correct force here.

It is precisely senseless therefore if, on the other hand, the atheistically minded part of the Socialists wish to demand as the basis of a future union of nations rather the preliminary removal of religion. Quite on the contrary, we say: if, for the different nations, an ordered community should exist, that can happen only by virtue of a principle which reaches far beyond the national life and is recognized as such a one even by the different nations. So what can that be? Only with Christianity is such a principle given because even Christianity teaches not only an original unity of mankind but also sets as its final goal a future reunion of the mankind at present torn apart into rival nations and therewith makes the effort accordingly a religious duty. One sees how federalism coincides here directly with the demands of Christianity, and is in this point, in general, nothing more than the worldly side of the Christian development itself.

But, in this way, all those who wish to be considered as the leaders of opinion of Christianity will recognize not only the task of international organisation in its full scope, but, at the same time, must enter forth for it according to their capacity. For, just as, on the one hand, the most comprehensive of the practical demands arising from Christianity lies therein, so, on the other hand, the one given most immediately. One may just glance at the actual origin of Christianity itself. If the age when Christianity could appear was first established by the Roman rule which brought the peoples together externally, we read indeed in the history of the apostles how on the Pentecost, with the founding of the first Christian community, also the inner community of the peoples emerged through a sudden removal of the dividing difference of languages. Therewith, from the start, the character of the Church was established as a community of belief destined for all peoples and this universality is expressly explained in the apostolic Creed. If now the Church is the real organ for the Christian ideas, it must openly also belong to their profession to impel the peoples or the governments themselves through instruction and admonition to work as far as possible for the founding of an international organisation.

It is not less obliged to that as, on the other hand, to the demand of social organisation. Both demands are correlates, as we also noted already, that without the former even the latter remains without prospect. Still further: if it lies in the essence of the social question that one must thereby go into a thousand details, which for that reason brings with it the danger of narrowing the mind, it is then precisely the international question which first gives the view the breadth without which great points of view are not to be assumed, and which therewith rises above all petty considerations. That one however may not lose oneself in empty generalisations, that is guaranteed once again by the consideration of the social question. In this way the two are inseparably bound to each other, and without the insight into this inner connection one will not be able on either side to aim at a thorough success, because one still does not raise oneself to the standpoint from which the task is first to be surveyed. Just as the eagle whirls in the wind only with both wings, but crawls on the earth with one.[36]

But just as Christianity is directed in general not to the state but merely to man and to mankind, so also the community of nations demanded as a consequence of Christianity cannot aim indeed at the future founding of the so-called universal state. A foolish idea to be rejected from the start which, in a certain sense, even ancient Rome sought to realize. But how has the ancient Roman Empire ended? No, the state can never become a universal institution, it remains in all circumstances a particular existence precisely as the concerned country and people in which it arose. Have we, however, already recognized the state idea itself as too narrow for the ordering of the German affairs, and how much less could it suffice where it is a matter of the entire Christian world? There the idea of an organisation hovering over the whole, armed with a compelling power, is altogether excluded. What it is a question of

---

36 [In the emergence of the Christian Socialists who are so-called at present, this is therefore a chief defect from the start that they thereby abstract altogether from the international question. And therewith these people wish to combat Social Democracy, which however has, as is well-known, an international trait which actually contributes to its strength, and indeed bestows honour even on it as it therewith - naturally in its own way - reveals nevertheless a sense for the international task. If one therefore wishes to oppose Christianity to Social Democracy, it must then be a Christianity which is directed with its demands as much to the civic society as to the society of peoples and states. Otherwise no respect will be granted to Social Democracy if it rather had the view as if high politics still extended beyond the Christian standpoint, and that one does not venture there, which however would mean denying Christianity itself. Or, did that not enter the world with the announcement "*In terra pax*", and wherein would the guarantee of international law indeed lie but in international organisation?]

is rather a union which itself, in accordance with its final goal, should not indeed aim at removing the existence of special nations in general, but bring in more and more a peaceful co-operation through a free federation.

But more precisely expressed, it is not however really the nations which would have to confederate themselves, but they can do this only as an organised body. In practice, therefore, it is a question of the state authorities, and how these are at present disposed and will act, that will clearly be conditioned very basically by the inner constitution of the states. The more indeed they are centralised internally the more brittle will they clearly show themselves externally, and the more they at the same time expand themselves the more does their egoism also grow. Just as the states then wish above all to care for themselves, so will they also believe to be able to satisfy themselves. One sees also here how closely the internal development is connected to the so-called foreign policy. Least disposed for federation are, therefore, great centralised military states which emphasize their army, and, should the eventuality arise, instead of striving for a peaceful balance of contesting interests through negotiations, rather reach at once for their sword. Material power extends for them over everything. And how natural - incidentally noted - that they, for that reason, show themselves most unfavourable to the Church development which would be most favourable with regard to a federative world order.

If now Christianity is not in general directed immediately to the state, but to man, the possessors and bearers of the state authority must however, insofar as they themselves believe in Christianity, feel themselves in any case also driven to conform to its practical demands and therefore also to promote the founding of a Christian international community. What disastrous consequences will it therefore have in this respect if the state authorities break off more and more all relations with Christianity since, then, in the same measure, disappear also the means with which one could work on their conduct from the Christian standpoint. Therewith the state interest becomes the sole regulator of politics and how could that ever lead to a peaceful international community, since rather precisely interest is the mother of so many conflicts? Moral bonds and ideal aims are required for that, and how little indeed does the talk of humanity and enlightenment mean if, on the other hand, religious impulses are dissolved. If the state society cannot already exist without religion, so much less the international society, for which there is no compelling power maintaining order.

To want to drive out Christianity from the political life and from international politics would mean finally nothing more than to work into the hands of the Jewry. Or what could it wish for more than that Christianity - which stands most in the way of its tendencies and hurts it, so to speak, at every step - if it were not indeed in general to be removed from the world, still would lose all practical significance for the public life? Especially also for the high politics which rather should be made serviceable as far as possible to the Jewish interest. And with what success the Jewry knows to actually carry this through the Berlin Congress has recently shown, in that it expressly forced on Turkey, as on the countries once dependent on the same and now become independent, the recognition of the Jewish civic rights. That means: that they indirectly forbade these countries - naturally in the name of humanity and enlightenment! - to take up any protective measures further against the Jewish exploitative system. Oh, the high diplomacy seems to have become decrepit and already childish, for precisely this also had been lacking - wanting to make the so-called Jewish emancipation an article of the European international rights!

1.

All of this premised, we enter now the practical task, the path to which has already been pointed out to us thereby. For, if it stands firm that the universal state does not need to be considered as the final goal of an international organisation but the federation of peoples which can naturally develop, strengthen, and expand itself only gradually, then the preliminary stages for that are formed clearly by the actual so-called alliances. That is: temporarily and *ad hoc* concluded alliances; whereas the actual federation is to be considered from the start as concluded for ever, and as it should serve persisting goals, so also possesses certain constant organisation for that.

From this viewpoint, then, there emerges before us first of all the so-called European great power system which indeed was originally in the real sense of the term a system of alliances. Emerging indeed from the coalitions against the revolutionary and Napoleonic France, it then attained at the Vienna Congress its formal constitution. Then, however, fallen for a long time now to inner decay, it has continued to exist still only purely from an external point of view. Nevertheless, it still expresses its after-effects in that, until today, not only the diplomatic practice is attached to it, but also the general political thought shows itself to be so involved and attached to it that it is to be considered as a self-evident matter which could not indeed be different. And the more idea-less now this system has, in the meanwhile, become, the more destructively does it work; to rise above which is now a precondition to attain to better viewpoints.

If we investigate, therefore, the nature of this European great power system, already its name reveals that it is concentrated in the idea of mere power, and therewith disregards as much historical and moral foundations as higher civilisatory goals. To be a power or to become one is here a goal in itself. But, insofar as different so-called great powers stand alongside one another, - to what will their striving above all be directed if not to the increasing of their means of power? It is illuminating how, therewith, the military rule as well as the financial rule is given, so that the entire development of the nations revolves finally round the barracks and stock-exchanges. To the monstrous armies and the monstrous military budgets corresponds the monstrous capital power of the Rothschilds. This is in no way a mere external and accidental parallel, it has arisen from the present conditions themselves, which indeed developed under this system.

There have always been more or less powerful states, the present-day great power system however seems to indicate to a certain degree a special form of states, just as the great powers also claim a special authority. They alone wish to have decided on the matters to which they think to ascribe a European significance. It is very clear that they thereby care in the first place only for their own interests, and even so clear that the states not belonging to the class of the great powers sink increasingly into insignificance. All smaller states are therefore threatened with downfall, insofar as they have not already actually sunk. What *ratio existendi* do they still have within a system for which power alone is important? They are therein as superfluous as small businessmen superfluous in an economic order in which only capital is important. Even this parallel is once again striking. But this only incidentally.

But is the downfall of the smaller states to be considered then as a matter of such indifference? History proves, on the contrary, that the smaller states show themselves on an average to be much more favourable for civic and political freedom than for the progress of culture, and have performed relatively more for it than the large states, than the great military powers especially. It is already *a priori* clear how militarism opens the most unfavourable prospect for the progress in freedom and culture. Now it is indeed carelessly said that, in the present-day progress of things, the small states do not have any future in general, but must then this progress of things itself continue to exist? It should continue to exist as little as the present-day rule of capital, but also, in the world of states, there must be to a certain degree a middle-class. Certainly, if the small states wish to support themselves merely on their particularistic glory, they are lost, they will become the prey of the much more intensive particularism of the great powers, of which already sufficient examples lie before us. If they wish to save themselves, that is possible only through a general federative system, which however can emerge only when the present-day great power system disappears.

Further, this system had the consequence, as natural as destructive, that it drew out the ambition of becoming a great power. Thus we saw how, in this view, the Sardinian desire to be great power bound itself with the Italian desire for a national state and therefrom arose the present-day Italian Empire, whose highest striving is now: to play the role of a great power and to be recognised in full form as a great power. What blessings that brought for the entire European civilisation may, in the meanwhile, be doubtful, and so much more certain and striking, on the contrary, what an upsurge European militarism assumed since then. And if we glance at Italy itself, - what is it with its great power dealings when, in the meanwhile, the great mass of the country people find themselves in the most needy and oppressed situation, and in general hardly 1/10 of the entire Italian people possesses the franchise and therewith active state citizenship, whereas the remaining 9/10 are ruled and exploited by a franchise-aristocracy of the worst sort?

Everybody knows in what inner connection, further, the German catastrophe of '66 stood with the founding of this new-Italian empire. But even the idea of the great power as such contributed its own character to it. For, if Prussia was indeed a recognized great power, it possessed however hardly the means to make itself really important also in this position. It bore - as Prince Bismarck says - an armour too hard for a small body, its great power character seemed threatened for the future, or it had to expand itself. Also quite right, the question is, only, why then did Prussia have to be thoroughly a so-called great power?

Now, it did not wish to stand behind Austria, and Austria was once again a great power which thereby did not seem to lack the material basis for such a position. But did we not see already in earlier observations what disastrous effects even the Prussian and Austrian great power situation has had for Germany, in that therein lay the impossibility of an energetic development of the German federation? For, once again: the great power system lets, in general, no federative system emerge. And especially for a natural shaping of Germany it must be the greatest hindrance, as indeed the fall of the former Reich was an actual precondition of the development of the great power system. For, without Austria and Prussia, it would not have been, but how would these two have been able to become indeed special European great powers so long as the old Reich still stood in power? Only the emergence of its downfall, beginning in the Middle Ages, made that possible.

In general, the present-day great power system had been alien to the entire Middle Ages. And it could not be otherwise, so long however as the entire Western Christianity felt itself to be one in the most important foundations of its development. Bound by the hierarchical organisation of the Church spanning the whole; bound by the great similarity of the state constitutions based on feudalism, as by the similar system of the knighthoods, guilds and corporations; bound by the common Latin education and scholastic science, as by the common artistic development which was attached to the religious cult and found its most striking expression in the Gothic extending from Scandinavia to Andalusia. In view of these common bonds so far-reaching and penetrating so deeply into all life-conditions, there lay no motive, and even the possibility of it would have been missing, that individual states or nations may have wished to establish themselves as independent great powers. Against such egoistic particularistic tendencies already the Holy Roman Empire which had the uncontested pre-eminence would have stood against, so that at that time only the Roman Emperor had the predicate, "Majesty". A concept which indeed was taken over from the ancient Roman history. Not however that the pre-eminence of this Empire had indeed meant the rule of the German culture - since it did not at all call itself the German Empire - but it had the pre-eminence for the reason that the universal ideas of the Middle Ages concentrated themselves in it.

Now, what introduced the dissolution of this situation was the following. In the material fields, primarily the trans-Atlantic discoveries, conquests, and colonisations, as a result of which the naval powers separated themselves from the continental powers, and on account of their colonial- and trade interests then fell into uninterrupted conflict among themselves. In the intellectual field: the awakening of national literatures, whereby the common ideas retreated before the national consciousness to the background; much more, however, the division of the Church. If the Western community of nations was dissolved by these three, individual powers emerged since then with the claim to preponderance, at first the Spanish-Habsburg power, then France. This desire for preponderance however permitted, on the other hand, the coalitions of balance, and from that emerged afterwards once again the system of great powers in immediate connection (as we mentioned above) with the coalitions against the Napoleonic rule.

Well then, if therefore this system itself arose only through the historical process, the great power system is consequently also only a historical category which, just as it once emerged and attained temporary importance, so also will and must disappear in the further progress of the development once again. Even already the facts prove clearly enough how the great power system has already dissolved itself in itself, and continues to exist only through an external scaffolding.

If in the beginning there existed a sort of collegiality between the great powers, so that they maintained among themselves at least a pathetic peace, whereby Europe remained spared for a generation from great wars, such collegiality ceased fully after the revolutionary disturbances of '48. In the Crimean War, as soon after in the wars of '59, '66, and '70, great power stood against great power. What did the system perform to hinder these wars? As little as it previously performed in the Oriental question, where, rather, the special politics of Russia and England alone were the decisive factors. And is not the non-intervention principle proclaimed for a long time to a certain degree the actual declaration of bankruptcy of the great power system? It has therewith become a nonsensical system. And so now the great task is to found a new system, that is, a really vital ordering of the European relations which first gives the positive basis once again to the international law which is at the moment lacking to it fully.[37]

2.

If the Middle Ages was the great thesis, through which, on the ruins of the world of antiquity, after the storms of the migration of the peoples, gradually a strong foundation of social and political order was once again acquired, the so-called modern history is characterised as the antithetical period. For, as in the Middle Ages universal ideas and tendencies predominated, so there entered afterwards rather more the special strivings and special interests of the individual nations and states into the foreground. If therefore the history of the Middle Ages must be comprehended as a whole, on the contrary it is, in general, impossible to give an actual total picture of modern history because there an inner community did not exist, but all strivings ran against one another mutually. What a long catalogue would it be to present all the oppositions that have emerged since then and are partly still effective today! In Germany it is present most immediately before our eyes, as certainly as an actually common development did not indeed take place amongst us for centuries, neither in the political nor in the intellectual field.

But, just as all things have their time, so also the antithetical period gradually waned once again. The modern history was followed by the contemporary, in which now the need for a synthesis makes itself increasingly valid. In the political field, the first expression of it was the former Holy Alliance.[38] That the same soon after became a pure hypocrisy

---

37 [I have treated all these matters in detail in the *Untersuchungen über das europäischen Gleichgewicht* already mentioned at other places.]
38 Alliance signed between Russia, Austria, and Prussia at Paris in September

does not however remove the fact that the presentiment of a higher condition was expressed therein. The wars of freedom, whose final result then seemed like a divine judgement had indeed shaken up to a certain degree the public consciousness. And - as mentioned shortly before - yet an alliance itself is the preliminary stage to an actual federation. In the intellectual field, on the other hand, we wish - as a sign of the beginning revolution - to remember only Goethe, in whom emerged so unmistakably the striving beyond the merely national to a world literature. And did not Byron also stand at his side insofar as he threw away the specifically English culture from himself and felt himself much more as a European? So much as a beginning.

If now it is a question of the foundation of a new community of nations, this can at first encompass only western Europe, as one which has had in the Middle Ages a common history, which, in spite of the national and political division which emerged thereafter, still left behind such deep after-effects that this entire territory of countries - vis-à-vis eastern Europe - even to today has preserved in the main points its inner relationship. A relationship which indeed becomes once again so much more striking in our days with the enormous upsurge of the means of communication, and makes the nationalistic tendencies, in spite of themselves, increasingly more important. Or one has to be blind not to see how the tendency to a uniform civilisation makes itself noticeable everywhere. If, however, this circle of peoples and countries on the other hand have lived through the antithetical period of the modern age, in which the peculiarities still undeveloped in the Middle Ages attained formation and self-consciousness, it can now also be a question only of a free union of these peculiarities. And even for that reason will the new situation be synthetical, for all synthesis presupposes an antithesis. If therefore the mediaeval ideal was a hierarchical organisation of the members, with the Pope and the Emperor at the top, the new ideal can only be a federation of independent members, and that with a polyglot formation, in opposition to the universal Latinism of the Middle Ages.

It is self-evident that such a federation cannot arise all at once. It requires at first a real basis on which it rests, and from which then even the impulse to it must emerge. Where would such a basis be found if not in Germany, whose federative determination we have sufficiently pointed out in earlier observations? Let us however add now that it is nonetheless

---

1815. This Alliance was gradually enlarged by the entry of almost every European ruler except, notably, the Pope and the Prince Regent. The Alliance insisted that "the precepts of Justice, Christian Charity and Peace --- must have an immediate influence on the Councils of Princes and guide all their steps".

Germany which suffered most under the fall of the former Western community, in that it, as a result of that, became a European battlefield, and sank from the high position that it assumed in the Middle Ages finally to a political nullity. And is it not obvious similarly how even the present-day militarism, which arose even from the lack of an international organisation, burdens once again Germany above all? But we add: if it was Germany from which the division of the Church emerged, which then contributed most to the fall of the community of Western nations, then Germany is, for that reason, above all obliged to enter forth for the new foundation of such, and therewith to prepare the way for the transformation of the entire European system for the better.

Truly, that would mean something different from the undertaking of '66, which itself emerged only from the ideas of the great power system, and has ensnared us only so much more again in this outmoded system! For it was not a question of making Prussia an effective great power or, let us say, the new Germany, for the moment the greatest European military power, which thereby panted under the burden which it therewith placed on itself, but of removing the entire great power bugbear from the world and making Germany the basis of a new system. That would have been first really a deed of political genius: laying the foundations for the development of the future! But what indeed was to be hoped for in the future, according to human judgement, in the creations of '66! If the Gospel says that one should not fill new wine in oid bottles, nor on the other hand patch up old clothes with new scraps, that is precisely what happened through the system of '66, and happens on the basis of it until today. An example of that: the so-called tax-reform through the tobacco-monopoly.

Finally, just as it is most obliged to that international task, Germany is most capable also for that, because, through its own religiously mixed population, it stands close to the Catholic as well as to the Protestant countries, and so forms the natural ground for the political balancing of this great opposition. I say for the political balancing, for it is in no man's power to remove the division of the Church in and for itself. The politician has to consider everything pertaining to that as given conditions which he cannot change nor may seek to change. So much more will he feel himself driven to overcome this opposition, at least in its political aspect, as the indispensable condition for the foundation of a new community of Western nations which, following everything, can emerge only from Germany.

But to recognize rightly what it is important in practice, we shall first have to observe even the present-day situation of affairs, after which finally even the significance of the whole will emerge so much more clearly.

Chap. XIX : Closing Observations

1.

Only great practical goals can elevate a nation. On this therefore will the rise of the German nation depend: that it recognize and energetically grasp its world calling. Until today that has not yet happened. But that it may happen, one must above all also be clear on what until now stood against it.

Nations develop slowly, this is true most perhaps of the German. And how would Germany now have been able, after a period of many centuries of progressive downfall, to raise itself in a short time to its former greatness? For a long time become incapable of an active participation in European politics, sunk through the inner splitting up into powerlessness, then for a time indeed robbed of its political existence, it was already a great thing that it won this back through the wars of freedom, at least in form. But Germany had not become thereby by far a living body. And far from it that one had raised oneself then to great political conceptions, the actual relations effected rather a new narrowing of the political horizon.

For, at first, it was the internal formation of the individual German states to which all ideas and strivings were directed. And indeed it was the German medium states and small states which entered into the foreground in this direction. What was won thereby in sense and practice, to move oneself in free constitutional forms, should remain unforgotten. But, in view of the great German total task, the medium- and small stately constitutionalism could only lead to the fact that one grew accustomed so much more to narrow conditions and lost the measure for the treatment of large political questions. How tangibly did that emerge in '48, when one wished, on the basis of all the ideas that one had formed in those spheres, to undertake the reorganisation of the German total body! Those were indeed quite incommensurable things and therefore the failures of that time inevitable.

If in the meantime there have not been lacking people who, unsatisfied with the constitutional instincts in the German particular states, demanded beyond that a total German development, they found themselves however in full ignorance of what that actually meant.

Namely, that it involved nothing narrower than a removal of the European great power system, as something which (as we think we have shown sufficiently) rather was based on the disintegration of the German total body. No thought of that, but precisely this great power system was now to form the support for the reorganisation of Germany. Therewith, however, there arose immediately the question: on which of Germany's two great powers does the new Germany have to lean upon? And what did that mean, taken in a basic sense, but to give up Germany in and for itself, when, instead of it, rather Prussia or Austria entered into the foreground? Thus dragged into this alternative, Prussia or Austria?, the German question was therewith totally falsified already from the beginning. And what indeed was to be expected from the new Germany that should rest on a Prussian or Austrian basis? For the German world vocation, in both cases, as little as nothing. That is shown by the simplest deliberation.

If the Austrian united monarchy has had, from its origin, a certain grandeur - a higher spirit, as in the Holy Roman Empire in its golden age, did not embody itself in this monarchy. Brought together through marriages and inheritances, and so a product of feudalism, that is, of a period of development in its downfall, this monarchy was accordingly directed rather to the holding on to the past than to the preparing for a new future. And so even the former Roman-German Empire became for Austria only a sort of heirloom which, to be sure, gave its possessor still a certain aura, and served as a background to far-reaching claims but did not for long possess the ideal force any more which would have been able to stimulate the minds to great conceptions. With the rule of Austrian culture over Germany therefore stagnation was produced.

The Prussian culture, on the other hand, seemed to offer quite different prospects. For that openly strove out from the past and was directed to the foundation of a new condition. But, in that it put aside the German past from itself, the great ideas at the same time disappeared from it which had lain at the basis of the former Reich. And how petty did the Prussian goals seem in comparison to that! For Prussia it was thought to be a great thing, to be sure, to acquire one little German land after another, but what does that indeed mean for the world-position of Germany, which was thereby only so much more led to its internal dissolution? Thus the Prussian history was perhaps a school of industriousness and love of order, a stimulus to refinement and an impulse to energy lay therein, but it could not direct the minds to high goals, it rather diverted them far from them. And accordingly we saw indeed how the present-day Prussian-German Reich, in which now the mind came to its mastery, which had developed itself through the history of the Prussian state, abstracts itself from the world-calling of the former Reich.

Only on the basis of the former federation still encompassing all of Germany would German-political ideas also have been able to develop themselves. Presupposing indeed that this federation itself had attained to a political activity, instead of which it remained in reality a merely passive body. If therewith there was lacking for such a development of ideas every real content, only science would have been able still to give the impulse to a higher conception of the German world-calling. Only, science itself held only a lack of awareness of that and increased the confusion of minds. For (as mentioned in its place) the understanding of the really German was in general lacking in the German scholars, therefore they indulged in theories which had no relation at all to the German problem. And so it is, even upto today, the poor conception of the so-called constitutional state which forms indeed the catch-word for the great politicising public, just as scholarly thought also turns around that.

7.

If now federalism has shown itself, in theory and practice, as a universal principle, it has however therewith at the same time yet a special quite immediate relation to Germany, whose federative disposition and determination was sufficiently demonstrated. That recognized, however, no true re-establishment of Germany is also consequently possible apart from its seizing energetically its federative calling, which is one and the same with its national calling. And, in the same measure in which this happens, the German nation - returning to its own nature from which it has become alienated for centuries - will then also emerge creatively into the institutions and undertakings in the field of public life, where it has for so long been only imitating and, until this day, continues to imitate.

For what would be originally German there? If we had borrowed the economic system ruling among us until now, just as the constitutional system of government similar to it, from abroad, the Socialist ideas also have come to us recently from there. And as regards the new German Reich - has it not been created according to half Napoleonic and half Cavourean maxims? Federalism, on the other hand, would be something German, just as also, on the other hand, only Germany would be capable of carrying out the same practically and of bringing it to universal validity, according to its inner nature and according to its world situation.

We add, besides, how therewith, at the same time, would disappear the unfortunate tendency of our scholars of indulging in theories which have precisely the least inward relation or applicability to the German conditions, but almost expressly emerge only as school wisdom, struck from the start with sterility for practical life. From the federative standpoint the opposition between theory and practice disappears, its significance is directed to both. Exactly as it appeared once among us in the case of our Leibniz, who should be the shining model for all German scholars. The striving towards universality essential to science suffered thereby so little damage that it rather found its vital impulse in the consideration of the affairs of the fatherland. For, as it considered Germany, and as the latter - even that we have shown not less – must be considered, so does the German question also acquire so much more of a universal significance the more deeply it is comprehended.

That indeed establishes first the true worth of Germany that its own development opens so manifold and far-reaching points of view as is to be said of no other country in the same measure. An external sign of that - that even today almost all the European dynasties originate from Germany, and a clear indication of the international calling of the same. But in this way we would recognize at the same time this: how, on the other hand, even the dissolution of the former community of Western nations, and then the rise of a political system according to which finally only actual force is still important, rests essentially on German events. It is a true statement therefore which Gentz[39] expressed two generations ago and perhaps of still deeper significance than the man himself imagined at that time:

"Europe has fallen through Germany, through Germany must it rise up again".

However, only federalism, which - as little as it may also at first signify at present -, is so much more the principle of political development of the future, can lead to this actually being realized.

---

39 Friedrich Gentz (1764-1832) began his career as a Prussian politician and later withdrew to publicistic activity. In 1802 he moved to Austria where he became the centre of the Conservative anti-Napoleonic agitation. He supported Metternich's policies from 1810 until 1830.

Chapter III

Edgar Julius Jung

The Rule of the Inferior, Part I: The Intellectual Foundations of Politics.

X: People, Race, Reich

The powerful representer of the mediaeval universe was Dante. His mind encompassed again with his ordering glance the entire divine and human government. From Plato to Augustine a straight path leads to the poet of the *Divine Comedy*. The great proclaimer of Christian human order was, however, at the same time the founder of the Italian vernacular, which eventually - oh, irony of world-history! - was to become the bearer of a self-conscious Italian national culture and ultimately of the idea of an Italian national state. With the fall of the Holy Roman Empire of the German nation came even earthly will to order, and political formative ability was lost to Christianity, as in the late Middle Ages the creative power of the Germans grew weary. Church-building may never enter in place of those historical powers which force men into legal and political forms, thereby first enabling a life of morality.

The more strongly Christianity was pervaded by humanism and cosmopolitanism, the weaker did the ordering force of Christianity become. Blurred concepts of happiness beguiled the fancy of the individualistic man. His suppressed impulse towards wholeness created for itself in wishful thinking that suprapersonal world to which he was never able in reality to penetrate, lacking genuine feeling of worth. The more often the hypocritical term of civilised humanity was used, the farther reality distanced itself from every true human community.

In place of the concept of Christianity there entered a blurred collective term, `humanity', which should be subjected to an examination here. First, one still understood by it basically only Western Christianity, since the expansion of ideas did not keep pace with the extension of geographical knowledge. But those men who sought out distant places stood on the ground of facts and differentiated with great harshness between Christians and heathens, between Europeans and subjects. The individualist thinkers of the 18th century, however, who created the foundations of the individualism ruling today, constructed a concept of humanity which ignored the factual. It did not take account of the deep-seated difference between the Western world and the remaining (the Eastern, the half-civilised and the barbaric) peoples. Thereupon came later, to establish confusion perfectly, an all-too cheap compassion for the coloured races. Negro children were endowed with European needs, which they indeed did not have, in a senseless transference of local relations to other climates and cultures. If this was the often condemned mistake of the 19th century, then the 20th century fell into a still greater one, the Negro cult, and drew from it impetuses for the dilapidated individualistic society. The misjudgement of true cultural values had to lead to weak ideas of compassion or to culture-endangering borrowings: genuine humanity sees other men, and genuine national culture other peoples only as the bearers of their cultural values. That weaker cultures fall to stronger ones is a fact of experience.

Above all, the complaint is to be made against the individualistic and social-political theories of Malthusianism, beyond all the varieties of Liberalism and Socialism, that its plans for human happiness are based on observations from some corner of the Western world or the other, and emerge from conditions of development which were taken in a hasty transformation. Whence came this overlooking of such basic things? From the illusions of erring thought which constructed humanity from a sum of detached individual persons without taking into account the reality: the peoples in their correctly differentiated ranking according to history, capacities, social and economic conditions, according to their climatic condition and attachment to a land. It dealt however almost always, apart from the idea of slave-emancipation, with goals present within the Western peoples, mostly with European ones.

A conscious limitation to the Western world or our history-pregnant part of the globe is therefore carried out by the author when he speaks of the people-ordering Reich. The overseas branches of Europe will already order their own relations, which are not nearly so confused. Therewith the question of the coloured races too is passed over. It forms the main concern of the colonial states. In South Africa, in Australia, one may merely recall in brief also the new racial type of South America, and point to the alleged approximation of the North American racial type to the Indian. The human-formative power of landscapes and continents is the great Unknown in every historical calculation.[40]

Thus, for the objective of this book, the most important thing remains a new ordering of the European mainland, of those countries which lie around the country of the centre, in the German historical region. This task is big enough, indeed absolutely overpowering, if one imagines to oneself how poor the German people just recently were in ordering thought. Even if the realm of financiers believes it can cross over the boundaries of the parts of the globe with impunity, even if industrial accumulations of an international sort are even today already successful, they do not change anything of the increasing division of Europe into ever new states, they do not prevent the progressing disintegration of the peoples into ever new unities, as we observe it among the North Germans, the Dutch, and the Anglo-Saxons. They do not change anything of the passions of the peoples: of the self-seeking wishes to lead, based fully on themselves, a national life independent in all respects. The ruling individualistic conception of the state is responsible for the failure of the national union founded precisely in this age as an ordering and arranging institution, which entered life when the last remains of the Western universal empire, the Austro-Hungarian multi-national monarchy, was destroyed by the same nationalities. Still the individualistic idea of the state with its deification of the national state seems to progress unstoppably, sharpening the oppositions and excluding every real ordering principle.

An end of this disastrous development is not to be anticipated so long as the individualistic idea of equality is simply transferred from individuals to peoples. Human rights are boundless, since everyone claims them. These human rights, however, are mechanically applied to groups, and soon every human conglomeration is explained as a "people". So to the anarchy of society corresponds, as a parallel phenomenon, the anarchy of peoples. Their egotism leads to battles of different sorts. In spite of the national union, in spite of many pacts, the

---

40 cf. C.G. Jung, 'The complications of American psychology', in *Collected Works of C.G. Jung*, Princeton, NJ, 1964, Vol.X, pp.509ff, where he points to the fact that the European human form has undergone visible changes merely through its adaptation to the new landscape, the `*spiritus loci*' of the American continent.

battle of all against all becomes, even in the life of the people, a lasting condition. Finally, only raw force produces something like a regulation of the communal life of the peoples, exactly as the police force in the individually decomposed internal states finally guarantees one more 'tolerable' order.

Nation, in the western sense, is a state-formed mass, not the destined and blood-related organism of a people: not within this, but within the state is the individual born. This western concept of the nation, from which the western idea of the state arises, stems from the Romance world. Even in the way in which the French impressed it, it appears to us inorganic. Its content is a double one: the state (with its boundaries, thus the ruling space) and the culture embodied in the vernacular of the ruling class; something is lacking in it compared to the national concept of all peoples with unbroken development: Germans, Slavs, Ugrofinns, indeed also the Celts. In these - this has also been argued by Fichte - continues to live the unbroken language and, therewith, national feeling. The Romance people, however, as descendants of the peoples subjugated and disintegrated by the Romans: as the remainder of the individualistic disintegration of the fallen antiquity, abandon the racially provided concept of the nation. The dialects of the languages emerging from vulgar Latin are, therefore, quite something else than the racially conditioned one of the central and eastern European peoples. It is not that the Romance peoples are more strongly mixed which differentiates from the already mentioned - for the latter are also mixed with one another - but the failure of racialism, the quite different constitution: the coloured blood which the Romans scattered over their entire empire from Asia and Africa is indeed also the reason that the Romance peoples accept coloured people without reservation in the state and society. The central European peoples, on the other hand, and the Anglo-Saxons, refuse the coloured people, even when they have desired equal political rights, connubiality and, therewith, full equal rights.

The Romance concept of the nation, which is inwardly therefore poorer than the national concept of peoples with an unbroken tradition, born in France, is thus naturally alien to German thought; as alien as the French idea of a national state. That the Germans cannot begin anything with it is to be gathered from the fact that every German scholar and writer constructs his own concept of the nation. Sometimes the decisive value is placed on the race, sometimes on the cultural community, sometimes on the state. Thus does Spengler[41] call a people which has

---

41 *[Der Untergang des Abendlandes]: Umrisse einer Morphologie der*

awakened in its entirety a nation. According to him, the people begin to be a nation when their feeling and thought begin to become historical. This pure difference of degree, however, does not enter the core of the question as it has been made evident here. The literature on the concept of the nation is immeasurable, the argumentation with it futile. In German, the word `nation' is to be abandoned without any further ado, thanks to the richness of our language and its capacity to put words together. `National people', `nation-ruling people', `people of the state', `the totality of the state citizens', `cultural nation', `language-nation',[42] and many other words allow one to clearly define, unequivocally, the concept meant at any particular moment. When one speaks of `nation', thus, only the French concept of *nation* should be meant.

From it stems the disastrous idea which individualism produced: the doctrine of the national state as the ideal- and model-organisation. Invented by a nation without an organic concept of the people, the national state does not naturally need to stop at the boundaries of foreign peoples. Its imperialistic striving crosses over them and is then forced, for the sake of inner equality and unity, to bring foreign cultures forcibly into line with its own nation. Such a national state which has national comrades outside the boundaries of the state can operate at the same time irredentically outwards and assimilatingly inwards. To the contractual constitution of the state of the naturally individualistic Romance peoples Fichte has already opposed the organic constitution of the state of the Germans, which, in the succeeding period, was taken up even by the Slavs and then, however, was developed wrongly under the influence of the French idea of the state.

The political impulse, the feeling-motivating phenomenon of the western state is called nationalism. Nationalism is not really - as a false linguistic image always expresses it - the rise of a moderate national feeling. It is, rather, the feeling arising from the idolisation of the state and related purely to the ideal of the state. Nationalism is something consciously impressed by the state, thus something artificially created recently, not an originally grown and unconsciously become thing. Different is the love for the fatherland and for one's people. It is rooted in the experience of the homeland, grows organically from the connection with the soil, blood and the spirit. It does not adhere to legal ideas of the

Weltgeschichte, [München: C.H. Beck,] 1918-23, [Bd.II], 2tes Kapitel, Abschnitt C.
42 `Staatsvolk, staatsführendes Volk, Staatsbevölkerung, Gesamtheit der Staatsbürger, Kulturnation, Sprachnation'.

abstract state. Thus, nationalism becomes a divisive power, an order-destroying passion.

These sharp differences of concept are only now in the process of becoming; the movement of renewal of the war-generation has not yet thought out this thought process in general to the end, even if it, directed by feeling, entered the right path: thus the concept of the "new" nationalism, to which the first edition of this book had held fast as well, was recently formed. The author has, in the meantime, attempted to follow the thought process of nationalism to its bitter end; he therefore turns away today from the misleading concept of nationalism.

Only superficial thought can reach the conclusion that thereby love for a people would be denied for the sake of their right and maintenance. On the contrary! The conscious turning away from the western idea of the state is only a necessary consequence of our history, since that intellectual world caused the rise of the west and of the German downfall. The rise of Germany again demands deeper ideas and ones suited to the German people, calls for more daring new spiritual creation for the purpose of the overcoming of German poverty of thought and German helplessness. The battle against individualism cannot be broken off simply at the idea of states and peoples. Even here the higher unity must be sought and, from it, the task of the part concluded. It is not fitting to preach the organic state and to remain stuck in the mechanical world-picture. If the idol of the individual falls, then too will that of individual people and therewith that of the idea of the national state. The individualistic thought of the equal rights of all nations must weaken that of the mission to which superior peoples within the community of peoples are called. A world-view which ranks the individual lower according to his worth must logically also strive, in the field of political new ordering and of the rights of peoples, to a greater and higher unity. Therefore we set against the self-seeking national state the entire land-encompassing Reich, a union joining together states, in which really free peoples entrust the leadership to the most suited people. "If we attribute to Germany, as a result of its Reich-character, the vocation not merely to form the passive central point of Continental politics but to intervene, actively ordering, in the international relations, as the guardian of the rights of the nations, as it were, that is certainly a very high calling" (Constantin Frantz). The transformation of the ideal of the national state into that of the Reich as the great life-form of the peoples is facilitated by the fact that we detach ourselves from feelings of inferiority which rule the present-day nationalists of the old stamp. It produced captivity, from it is explained the nationalistic isolation of German national circles. Neither the individual superior man nor the individual superior people fears free competition with others. Both are conscious of their worth and develop genuine mastery. Thus awakens in them the courage to believe in supranationalism, which has nothing to do with a disgraceful denial of one's own culture or cosmopolitan pallor. Thus grows from our anti-individualistic attitude, beyond the internal German tasks, the feeling of an international political mission to rescue the Western cultural circle from destruction: to become bearers of rechristianisation and, instead of anarchy, to set up spiritual, social and political unity. The Reich of justice, built on the idea of ranking and installing the peoples according to their worth and their cultural accomplishments, enters in place of the empty illusions - freedom, equality, fraternity and humanity. We do not wish to dissolve, but to bind. Bind through order, which thereby becomes the saviour from the chaos.

Tense emphasis of the national state (chauvinism) betrays a lack of deeper racial rootedness. The external belonging to a state does not lend security of life but the participation in the innermost being of a culture. Only it opens the possibilities of activity to fulfil oneself as a man and to participate in the striving for perfection of moral humanity. It would therefore be substituting the "new nationalism" with the concept of the idea of national culturalism,[43] if the latter did not have the overtone of the merely negative and of race-snuffling. National cultural is the striving to grasp the essence of one's own people to the last detail and to work for its realisation, thereby serving the mission of the people. This conception, which only includes affirmation in it and in no way a denial, should have been preserved in order to endow the word-formation "national cultural", in and for itself accurate, with triumphant penetrating power. What happened instead of that has been the overexploitation of a valuable idea, delivering it almost to falsification.

National culture is the strongest metaphysical connectedness of the individual man. His inner being is determined through the community of the political, social and cultural history. Soil, blood, and destiny are the melting-pot from which the formed nation emerges. Fichte calls a nation "the entirety of men living with one another in society and constantly creating themselves from themselves naturally and spiritually which, by and large, stands under a certain special law of the development of the divine out of it". God thus individuates Himself into a national culture, just as a man also is born without his will into the nation culture. Wilhelm

---

43 I have translated "völkisch", in this context, as "national cultural" to distinguish it from "rassisch", the connotation given to it by the National Socialists, but not always by the Neoconservatives.

Stapel,[44] therefore, says correctly: "We men can only recognize this our natural reality. One who revolts against this becomes unholy, and even if only in the warped nature of his soul, for he revolts against the will of God. Happy is he who is glad of what he is, for he fulfils the will of God. The denial of one's own national culture is basically inner godlessness, indeed hostility to God. - He, however, who declares his faith in the national culture from which he is sprung, will find it natural that even the other person is glad of his national culture. - Thus, from attention and care of national culture, racial hatred is never born, but a free, open life beside one another, even perhaps a life of mutual communication of the peoples".

The task of the naturally given national culture which is to be morally justified is only thinkable in those quite isolated exceptional cases, when the fusion of an individual into another culture from religious belief results in a personally painful decision. It is characteristic of these "noble renegades" - such as a H. S. Chamberlain or many passionately germanised Jews[45] - that they consciously sacrificed their national culture to one experienced as higher with the religious zeal which Christ demanded when he ordered the disciples even against familial bonds. However this sacrifice is obviously completely different from a mere surrender.

The return to vitality demands a stronger emphasis of the living organisms and the repelling of legal organisations. National culture is a spiritually bound-, the state is a legal form. Certainly, law is the ordering expression of metaphysical power. But it is more strongly allied to the world of the useful than to that of the feeling. Individualism has divinised the state in order to give it precedence over the people. The murder of the vital through the mechanical was the result. Today the peoples arise and strain against the chains of a state which threatens their right to existence. In place of the unconditioned precedence of the state must therefore enter the doubling of the state and people, or of Reich and peoples, which

---

44 Wilhelm Stapel (1882-1954) [*Antisemitismus und Antigermanismus*]: *über das seelische Problem der Symbiose des deutschen und des jüdischen Volkes*, [Hanseatische Verlagsanhalt, Hamburg,] 1928. Stapel was a member of the neoconservative circle and a supporter of the Nazi movement as well. His nationalistic publications include *Volksbürgerliche Erziehung*, Jena, 1917 *Der christliche Staatsmann: eine Theologie des Nationalismus*, Hamburg, 1932.
45 most notably, Friedrich Julius Stahl (1802-1861), legal philosopher and politician who had a marked influence on the direction of Prussian Conservative politics. He converted from Judaism to Lutheran Christianity in 1819.

receives its living expression through the constitutions.

The conception of the nature of national cultures represented here often meets, since it is supposedly Romantic, brusque rejection; and this, although the Romanticist Herder exerted an influence on the Slavs of eastern central Europe which helped in a very real way to form modern history. Especially Spengler wishes to carry out a separation of the natural and spiritual, of race and national culture. "One will however not understand even the history of higher mankind, if one overlooks that man, as the element of a race and as the possessor of a language, or man insofar as he originates from a uniformity of blood and insofar as he is classified into a uniformity of understanding, and, therefore, the existence and development of a man have their special destinies. - There are therefore currents of existence and bonds of development. - All the currents of existence have a historical, all bonds of development a religious stamp". This conception of history does not need to be investigated in this context for correctness or error. Existence and development flow together in the national cultures. Immediate feeling and consciousness make up the spiritual whole. Historical and religious stamping therefore cannot be separated. The direction of this work is rather towards the reacquisition of unity through metaphysical power: its guarantor is national culture.

Modern history is determined by the great peoples. However there are no great peoples who are racially pure. They are all somehow racially mixed. The mixture itself is less investigated and shrouded in mystery. Precisely the increased observation which racial questions have found recently indicates how very suprasensual things have risen in the general observation. For, here it is a question of connections which are temporarily closed to human knowledge. They are therefore not to be obtained through biological laws alone. As little as the relatively young racial research has led to conclusive results, so little can it be denied that the racial connection of the peoples has remained not without influence on their historical development and cultural achievement. The downfall of ancient cultures was certainly partially due to racial disintegration. The Negro question occupies the American public in a measure which has found race-protective expression through the immigration law of the United States. If therefore not only among the German people, but almost everywhere, the call for maintenance of racial purity and high breeding resounds, that is likewise a part of the confrontation between inferiority and superiority. If it is true that certain races demonstrate a special disposition to develop spiritual powers, the German people must strive to strengthen this essential racial component. The Nordics are to be considered as such today. On the worth of the remaining races, from whose mixing with the Nordic the German people has emerged, still less can be said. That less valuable integral racial components must be weakened or at least may experience no strengthening is perhaps plausible. In any case, caution, in view of the present-day condition of the racial doctrine and of the possibility of fallacies, is advised. Where are sure marks of purity of race? Leading racial researchers speak of the dark men with a Nordic soul. In turn, today serious reservations are made valid whether remnants of the Nordic race really represent such a valuable heritage. The lack of children and the political self-sufficiency of predominantly Nordic peoples (Sweden) arouse justified doubts. Further, we know very little of the connection between races and constitution types, of changes of inheritance (mutations). It is also dangerous to transfer to a people the discord of a division according to racially superior and racially inferior. Where is an adequate proof that the special predispositions, for example, of the Nordic race would raise the entire heritage of the German people in its racial possessions? Who presumes to characterise and to select the best breeding animals as such? Who can prove that the Nordic soul is really bound to the characteristic of the Nordic body? And who finally dares to include the implementation of a purposeful breeding in the realm of the possible? Man is not a domestic animal which can be bred, at least spiritual man. For, breeding is something that is through and through understanding-oriented. If "Eros" does not lead instinctively to an unconscious selective breeding, the coolly calculating understanding certainly cannot take the place of the deficient feeling for superiority. A human race grows; an estate on the other hand can be bred (the nobility).

What, however, is in no way appropriate is to want that disastrous effort of biology to judge all of history only from the point of view of the question of race. This is a materialism of the blood, a denial of the spirit, which makes it impossible to consider history as the field of free activity. If all men are only prisoners of their blood and their heritage, then every sensible striving for genuine freedom stops, then only the races need to be improved, and all else comes by itself. This conception of history is of course contradicted by itself, because it seeks to bring forth with calculating breeding that freedom of deed which is the significance of all humanity. One cannot however preach free decision in the same breath with the blood-related connectedness of everything spiritual. That is a contradiction in terms. "The German culture lies in the mind, not in the blood" (Lagarde).

Nevertheless, the fact of more valuable and inferior races remains, and from it follows the demand to protect the valuable. Race-protection from the consciousness of one's own worth is therefore a really acceptable venture for the political life. It should however have in view the great racial differences and not the small ones within the German people.

In no way, however, may the racial question become the bone of contention of politics; the rights of the individual citizens cannot be ranked according to racial points of view. To this aims that orientation which conceives the battle for inner renewal of German culture only as one of such "pure-blooded" Germans against the Jews. The racial question however has here only a background significance: in fact, people stand against people, mind against mind. What is racially conditioned in the oppositions of peoples has nothing to do with the supposed conflict between Aryans and Semites. The Aryan and Semitic races begin slowly to cross over from the field of linguistics, in which they originated, into the realm of myth. Spengler points out rightly that the Jewish race formed itself first in the ghettos of the West, and indeed through psychological breeding under very hard external conditions. The so-called Jewish race is thus not an original race, but a breeding, just as the Western aristocracy is a breeding. Perhaps on this circumstance is based the deep aversion of the Jews to feudalism. Here genuine races stood against each other, which forced one into the ruling position, and the other into particular quarters of the cities. Nevertheless one can hardly speak of a uniform maintenance of the spirit of the Jewry, since even it - this will be entered into further below - decomposes into different camps. It is correct that the Jews inhabit predominantly the camp of individualism. Seen from the standpoint of this book they are reactionaries who, by and large, hold fast to a world-view which must be overcome. The Jews are individualistic and thereby the people of collectivism. They have little understanding of the Faustian battle for inner freedom. The heroic as well as the tragic does not find a place in them - not considering the heroic attitude of many individuals. The idea of immortality, a demand of the practical reason in Kant, is transferred, among the Jew, from the metaphysical to the this-worldly. He abandons the immortality of the soul in the Western sense only to exchange it for the immortality of the self and the people. Berdiaev remarks that the Jewish myth belongs typically not to the past, but to the future; it is the eschatological myth.[46] It concerns the passionate demand of a thousand-year kingdom of God on earth, the judgement day, on which the good finally triumphs over the evil and justice will be established. Socialism

---

46 cf. Berdiaev, *Christianity and Anti-semitism*, N.Y.: Philosophical Library, 1954.

too, which is to be traced to Jewish sources, amounts to that. In Karl Marx, a typical Jew, all this again finds expression; even his Socialism expects earthly justice and blessedness, and he transferred the messianic idea to the class of the proletariats which should free the world from injustice. "The Jewish history is the revelation of God in the fortune of men, whereas the pagan-Aryan religions were revelations of God in Nature".

He points also to the passion and intolerance of the Jewish people which is explicable from this religious situation. There can indeed be no doubt that the Jews, who could reach a so far-reaching position of power in the West only on the basis of the Liberal demand for tolerance, in fact tend towards intolerance. No people tolerates so little genuine and justified criticism. Stapel therefore once set the anti-Germanism of the Jews against anti-Semitism.[47] In fact! The maintenance of the Jewish type is the good right of this long-living and tough people which has brought about, through its this-worldly messianism, a very astonishing power of collective self-maintenance. It is only the question whether, in the long run, a minority people may and can force its intellectual condition on the numerically much stronger host people. Today the Jews hold this intellectual position of power and defend it with a force which must produce counter-effects. For, it does not contradict in any way the recognition of equal rights for the Jews if a people wish to be ruled only by their own kind, thus preserving their racial sovereignty. "It is the natural right of every people that they wish to know their fate ruled according to their own instincts" (Stapel).

The position of the Jews among the Germans is to be comprehended only when not only their blood-related and spiritual determination, but also their social position is included in the sphere of considerations. The Jews could overcome the armour with which the Western society of the Middle Ages, divided according to estates, had protected itself only in two forms: either in that they penetrated the essence of the social structure of the West to the last detail and submitted to its conditions of rise, or that they destroyed the existing society. The Jew had to become German, English or French, etc. He became Anglo-Saxon; apparently because the numerical influx into England had already been checked and sifted. Perhaps also for the reason that the social armour of the conservative English people was so strong that only an adaptability to them and not their permeation could lead to success. It is otherwise in the case of the German people, whose central situation was

---

47 Stapel, *op.cit.*

at the mercy of the chief thrust of Jewish immigration to the West. Here the onslaught succeeded so impetuously, here the social armour was already so undermined that the Jewry could reach their goal in a revolutionary way and method. The Jew needed only to seize the party of the Enlightenment and of individualism, and to erode from inside out the edifice of the German social structure. Thus he did not need to work his way up to the top of society, but he forced on the Germans a conception of society which had to lead the Jewry to towering heights. The catchwords, equal worth and equality, became a magic key which opened all closed doors. "If for the European-American democracy the constitutional battles and revolutions meant a development towards the ideal of civilisation, they are for the Jew the destruction of all that is different from him" (Spengler).[48] The attitude of the Jews has thus become revolutionary among the Germans and their union with the proletariat natural. The present-day Jewish attitude is only understandable through the anxiety to become once again socially "suitable". The resentment of the ghetto determines in this way even the future attitude of the Jewry.

The battle has been won for the Jewish people. They have triumphed and no one seems capable of making this victory disputable. To be sure, only so long as the Germans remain bound to an individualistic conception of society and politics, confirming in this way the prerequisites under which alone the Jewish position of power is durable. If, therefore, the 20th century will bring the great debate between individualism and the organic world-view, if we have already crossed the threshold of a new age, then the Jewish question will be opened anew. It is to be expected that the Jews hold fast in a predominant majority to individualism, indeed even remain the main supports of this front. Now, it is certain that the German soul, if it is still unharmed, will win in this battle, even if the German Jewry should persist in its western attitude. The question is, whether it does that. To pose this question means to trace it back to a still more difficult one: whether the Jews are individualists by virtue of their blood and religion or by virtue of their history; whether inner intellectual constitution or historical resentment determines their present-day attitude. If the former is correct then an adaptation to German culture - considered as a whole - may be impossible. There remains then space for only one development, which assigns to the Jewry the position of a racial minority. If his individualism has only historical causes, then,

---

48 Spengler, *Der Untergang des Abendlandes*, Bd.II, Kap.III: `Probleme der arabischen Kultur', Abschnitt C: `Pythagoras, Mohammed, Cromwell'.

today after the full Jewish self-emancipation, an adaptability to the spirit of the host people is thinkable. So much stands firm: the role of the person differentiating himself from the other citizens of the state only through his religious confession is to be maintained only so long as the national culture rooted in the suprasensual is no longer considered as a foundation of the state, but as a sum of individual men who accidentally have their habitation within the state boundaries. The moment, however, when the peoples of the West begin to be conscious of their innermost nature, the question is no longer about the difference of confessions, but of national culture.[49] A double national affiliation is to be drawn into the realm of the possible only in quite isolated cases, only among boundary peoples with a special fate. But even this possibility is resolutely denied by the recent science. The Jewry itself indeed reveals a direction which, on the one hand, goes back to the depths of religious sources and, on the other hand, is infected with the national cultural awakening of the Western peoples: Zionism, the national cultural movement of the Jewry, is nothing other than a blossom of this intellectual spring of national cultures. There are in it unbelievers who hold on only to the national culture, and orthodox believers to whom it has to do with religious rebirth. It seems therefore as if not inconsiderable parts of the Jewry carry out the logical turning away from individualism: one to their own Jewish culture. This development must - if one overlooks the emigration to Palestine - lead to a classification among the racial minorities. The chief camp of the German Jewry however rejects Zionism, without at the same time jumping in with their heart in their hand into the German culture. Whether it can, in general, do this nobody perhaps will be able to answer. Spengler maintains in this regard: "But even if the Jew considers himself as a member of his host people and participates in its fate, as it was the case in many countries in 1914, he does not still experience it, in fact, as his own fate, but he takes sides with it, he judges it as an interested onlooker, and precisely the final significance of that which is battled for must remain always closed to him".[50] Even this greater part of the Jews is not enclosed in itself: it consists of orthodox people, Liberals, and atheists who perhaps adhere closely to the German people but remain, according to their consciousness, Jews. What will happen tomorrow is unknown.

---

49 Eugen Dühring (1833-1921) in his *Die Judenfrage als Racen-, Sitten- und Culturfrage*, Karlsruhe, 1881 (posthumous 6th rev. ed., 1930), claims to be the first to have considered the Jewish problem as a racial and cultural, rather than a religious, one.

50 Spengler, *Ibid.*.

Today the non-Zionist section of the German Jewry persists in an international attitude: "The historical fate has driven the Jews into the many state unions. Therefrom grows the task for them of working towards a peaceful total organisation of the world. For, for the Jews, every war between peoples is a war between brothers in the real sense. The Jew is therefore the born pacifist, fate has assigned pacifism to him as a world mission".[51] The German people also want peace; but not for the preservation of Jewish interests, but of their own. Never, however, can they become basically pacifist, because their development, their freedom could be limited by it. Without freedom, a people die; the German dies for freedom. For him, therefore, war is not, as for the Jew, always a crime. Finally, there still remain the Jews striving for full assimilation, of whom it is uncertain whether they could ever do what they want, namely become German. If, finally, one disregards individual Jews who are not Jews any more - there are such cases in all racial groups - then the Jewish question remains a black cloud on the horizon of the future. However, so long as the war of the world-view rooted in the suprasensual against individualism is not yet carried through and especially the attitude of other peoples to the work of freedom of the new German generation is not yet cleared, every plan for a state regulation of the "race question" is immature. Measures for the raising of racially valuable components of the German people and for the prevention of inferior currents must however be found today rather than tomorrow.

The turning away from individualism brought the rediscovery of national culture. Even so the idea of race protection arises from suprasensual thought. The present-day anti-Semitism on the other hand cannot deny its origin from an individualistic world-view. All its characteristics point to it. External race traits had to serve for it as the foundation of the judging of intellectual questions. Therewith it subscribed to a biological materialism. Scientifically overcome doctrines of a Lombroso were taken over into the field of racial research. Of course, the marketable anti-Semitism also raised the demand for the renewal of the German racial spirit; practically, however, indeed on account of its individualistic origin, it did not know how to shape such a renewal. For it, the renewal is produced always in the pure combating of

---

51 [Eduard Bernstein, quoted from Stapel, *l.c.*] Bernstein (1856-1932) was a Jewish Socialist politician of the Weimar Republic. In his *Von der Aufgabe der Juden im Weltkrieg*, Berlin, 1917, he encouraged the establishment of a new Internationalism based on the universal dispersal of the Jews and their characteristic internationalist ideas.

the Jews. As if the German people had not opened the door and gate themselves to individualistic thought and therewith to the Jewish influences. He who himself remains in his very soul Liberal can, to be sure, reach only two possibilities: either of seeing in the Jew only the German of another faith, or of suppressing him with raw force. It requires therefore no more proof that both ways are equally impossible. Against the first stands the racial will to self-assertion of the Jews, against the second the moral law. But even the instrument of the war of anti-Semitism is individualistic; it betrays its imprisonment in the intellectual realm fundamentally attacked by this book. This is proven by the spiteful ways of battle between individuals, where it however is a question of disastrous oppositions between racial spirits; but then also of the stirring up of coarse material passions which, like Marxism, wishes to make envy the guiding principle of all politics.

The new attitude to the questions of the national culture and race characterised here signifies a declaration of belief in population policy (true politics of the people), on which a separate part of this book will elaborate. In place of the sole concern for the individual citizen of the state - a concept of the present-day politics - enters the care of the national cultural body, the striving for its maintenance and purity. For, if the new generation sees once again the divine in man, it must feel the German culture as the earthly vessel in which the divine and moral content is held. This culture therefore we wish to know secured and without end; we want to see it grow and develop itself. We are ready to sacrifice ourselves for it. So that it can maintain itself, we wish it power, but conceive this power only as a duty in the service of the eternal tasks of man.

Therewith have been pointed out the final values, towering above the individual existence, which must be protected and preserved, if the significance of life should not be destroyed. These values are unshakeable and not transformable, their essence is based on the entirety of the human reason, on the operation of the macrocosmic world. Among falling idols, the new man raises again his yearning eyes to God. He obtains once again eternal values, a law enthroned unchangeably, to which he subjects himself. The impulse to maintain such values at any price, insofar as it streams out to the life of culture, of the society and of the state, is conservative in the highest sense of the word. Thereby is outlined the minimum of conservative preservation which every people must summon forth in order to elude self-destruction. At a moment when life has fallen into ossification, the sources of metaphysical powers seem to be submerged, the `cocoonisation' constantly progresses, and the disintegration of human society into a visible process of crumbling has begun, there is for the rescue of vitality, of morality, of true personality, only one attitude promising rescue: the conservative. Once the progressive direction may have had its significance: as ossified forms, they must be broken up in the name of life. But since all the chains have fallen, the progressive attitude is a push towards emptiness or suicide. In this last sense has the great age of preservation, of conservatism, begun.

Far from us, however, lies every conservatism which would like to maintain external and surviving forms. The present-day forms of society and state are, in the real sense of the word, indeed not forms any more; they are empty burnt cinders, evidences of formlessness and of the process of decomposition. To hold fast to them would mean to pay homage to that disreputable conservatism which clings to conditions instead of fulfilling itself in the spiritual. These conditions however are ripe for a downfall.

We have obtained something which rules over us as an unshakeable law: what goes beyond the cognitive power of the individual man can not be touched by human self-will. But because we have established once again and limited anew the realm of the holy, we have freed ourselves from the demon, recognizing false transitory values in their nothingness. We are evolutionists in the purest sense of the word: spiritually and intellectually we overcome a world become rotten and transform its values, because the highest value remains unshakeable for us. If this transformation of all values leads also to a radical change of things, then we may also call ourselves revolutionaries. The revolutionary attitude however is valid only for the external circumstances of this fragile social edifice. In fact we wish to end the 400 year-old individualistic revolution of the West and to introduce a creative age of preservation. The way to this goal is war. Our justification is: that one must - from the deepest will to preservation - destroy. True worth demands the destruction of unworthiness.

Thus arises, rejuvenated from the ashes of a war burying an age the German man, new life, and new order, but proclaiming the eternal God.

Part VI: Foreign Policy.

V: National cultural foreign policy

The constant preservation of the same direction is guaranteed only when the sense for the higher purposefulness of the existence of the people has come alive once again. Then the political instinct awakens to new life. Leaders arise who balance their own will to the popular will. The significance of the national community in the scope of the world-view resting in the suprasensual has already been made clear. The nation is, to it, the earthly individuation of the divine being, in which the individual himself may continue to live. If God reveals Himself to the individual man, it is only in the spiritual form which is conditioned by the special spiritual condition of his own people. Thence the significance which the person obliged to the communal worth attaches to national culture: he wishes to acquire the vessel in which he may continue to live the divine being which has become manifest to him.

Besides, however, he recognizes also the necessity of an order towering above his own people. The total experience obliges him indeed not to work for a mere concept of mankind of the individualistic sort but for the creation of a higher order in the life of the nations, in which the entirety is glimpsed, at first of the peoples of the same territory and interconnected history. In the chapter, "People, race, Reich" the philosophical foundation for this demand has been given.

Since the intellectual concept of culture is bound to the physical aspect of the people, there follows therefrom the affirmation of the self-maintenance and security of the national existence as the first law of life. But even attention to foreign peoples. Besides, however, the German recognizes the special position of his people in every advanced spirituality, which calls the German people to make the next step to human perfection: to the establishment of a right legal order among the peoples, at first of the European territory, in his immediate neighbourhood. Charity begins at home. Human perfection however means the approximation of man to the divine and the distancing from the barbaric. Thereby the striving for perfection remains a goal in itself, the goal eternal and unattainable. From the recognition of the German duty towards humanity grows the feeling of a mission. The insight that national culture as such must be developed freely and unrestrictedly in order to be able to serve really as a vessel leads, in connection with the consciousness of a special task, to the pressure to create for this culture a spiritual leadership role among the other nations. That is not overconfidence, which leads to presumption, but a necessary impulse to the furtherance of spiritual development. If lower self-seeking utilitarian instincts work against this effort, the German is obliged to counter them. He must fight for the validity of his culture, if necessary even under sacrifice of his own life. Therefrom are effortlessly produced two foreign political directional points for our age:

The entire German people is to be made the foundation even of its political thought and existence; it must strive for the position which is suited to its spiritual powers and necessary for the exercice of its missionary vocation. Only then do unequivocal foreign political goals arise from intellectual facts, from the basic spiritual attitude, consciously in the case of the leaders, emotionally in the case of the entire mass of the people.

The way to these goals is conditioned by circumstances which prescribe a quite definite direction. For a people does not stand, as a spiritual vessel, to a certain degree in a void. But it is bound and linked to the destiny of the earth which it shares with other peoples, whose fate is more strongly connected to it than the individualistic way of observation recognizes.

The German people holds the centre of Europe. In the north, west, and southwest of the settlement area of the Germans live - round the centre of Europe - "old" peoples, almost entirely with national states of the western stamp: mostly with clear national and linguistic borders. (The political borders have, to be sure, advanced since 1919 over the German national territory). In the northwest, east and southeast of the German settlement area on the other hand - still within the inner European territory - the peoples are interlinked to one another in terms of settlement. Here there are no border lines of peoples, but broad, simply drawn borders of contact. The political ideas of this territory must therefore be different, more mobile, corresponding to the situation. If the pre-war solution of the problem of peoples and states was already unsatisfactory in this mainland territory, still more so the present-day one. Here in the heart of Europe a powerful task of resolution persists: to find new forms for the living together of the mainland peoples who lack clear territorial borders.

That is the prime task of the Reich German foreign policy which has for the time being only to act in the west and remove the mistakes of the Versailles Treaty as much as possible. For the moment the German people has nothing to offer the west, unless indirectly through the west. There lies the key.

These - in no way new - national and territorial political foundations of the German foreign policy were ignored and therefore forgotten by an instinctless age inclined to illusory ideas which considered only the individual peoples. Thence the collapse of German foreign policy and the lowering of its perspective, therefore its lack of tasks and direction. The foreign political thought of the pre-war period however was conducted only in states and not in peoples. It was not based on the enclosedly settled Germans in Central Europe, but only on "the inhabitants of the Reich", who however were only a part of the entire German people - at the borders besides mixed with foreign peoples - and also not on the territory which the entire people inhabits and on the radiations of this territory and of the entire people.

Here lies a goal of the highest significance which perhaps the materialistically thinking person grasps partially when he arrives through different ways at the understanding of the Great-German-Central European. Foreign policy must be interlocked in the people and the soil, the idea of the political union of all German culture and of the mastery of the German cultural soil must therefore be basic. German foreign policy must therefore strive in two ways, in terms of the people and in terms of Europe:

for the Germans, who live in Central Europe on the closed national soil: a political entity of "Germany", which there is not yet today; for the Germans outside Great Germany: living space, that is, secure self-rule of its national cultural affairs within its host state,

for Europe: new order beginning with the central, near eastern and near south eastern territory and progressing from there to the borders, in the form of a European states union.

Both goals are more closely linked to each other than a fleeting examination allows one to suppose. They embody the idea of the historical Reich in its present form suited to the present circumstances. For the same right to a national state and to security of the foreign positions not encompassed by this must be granted even to the remaining peoples of the same territory through an international legal order.

The complaint that the setting up of such far-reaching goals in this time of German powerlessness is without a prospect of realisation is false. If powerful performances are demanded of the German people, even a great thing must be held in view. Victor Hugo, imprisoned in the forms of French political thought, swore, on the occasion of the transactions of the National Assembly at Bordeaux on the Frankfurt Peace of 1871, the reconquest of Alsace-Lorraine, Mainz and Cologne! Only one who wishes the entirety makes great efforts. Giving up from the start and lack of a goal lead to the background. Moreover anything else is impossible. For colonial and overseas policy is unattainable while these goals are to be justified ideologically, historically and economically. The inner lack of peace and the economic situation of Europe cry directly for a new order.

Public declaration of still more far-reaching goals of foreign policy does not only frighten. It also conceals advantages. Even enemy policy can prepare itself on clear political lines. That is proved by the success of Japan, when in the nineties proclaimed much more wide-ranging and thereby really self-aggrandizing goals. Uncertainty on goals dissatisfies more strongly in the long run: it spreads mistrust, because no foreign statesman can calculate what will happen if unexpected new events enter. That was precisely the most terrible mistake of the German pre-war policy.

VI: The national cultural goals

Two states, the present-day Reich and a coming state of all Germans in the central European closed settlement area, one of which would encompass sixty-five, the other however almost eighty million Germans, are different from each other in terms of their strength not only numerically. The inner forces of a community indeed do not grow merely according to the number of people, but in accordance with the increasing multiplicity of the intellectual talent of the individual parts. Large Germany would in comparison to the present-day Reich perhaps increase its population by half, but certainly not by a quarter, as the arithmetician thinks.

In addition, there is the significance of space. German Austria brings in the reunion with the Reich not only 6 million Germans but also the Alpine countries which open their bends far towards the east and the middle Danube. In the knowledge of the high significance of such an increase of power, the victorious power-holders forbade the reunion in 1919. Slow Switzerlandising was to be the fate of the Austrians: they were encouraged to form their own new national culture split off from German culture and to have joy in an independent political existence which the people had expressly rejected in 1918 through a concurring determination of the National Assembly. Economically, Austria is not once again to be bound to the states of the Danube basin. The once sadly rejected Danube Federation is today offered as a "Central Europe without the German Reich" by the Czechs: Austria would then be separated finally from the Reich, which therewith would be cut off from the lower Danube. All attempts to delay or to push behind the political union between Vienna and Berlin - no matter whence they come, what means they use, and under what masks they appear - are to be combated as hostile to Germany. Placed by itself, the politically powerless and economically non-viable Republic of Austria - as the booty-aim of foreign populated neighbours - is a source of danger for the German people, but also for the German Reich and for Europe.

The reunion would bring no new dangers to the Reich: the Reich indeed has - as the correspondence between Stresemann and Mussolini revealed in 1926 - inherited already all the annoyances arising from feeling (imponderabilia) of the former Habsburg state. It is important now to draw also the benefits. Then Upper Silesia, which threatens to be constricted in the south by the Czechs, in the north by the Poles, will be relieved; for, the Czech state would be surrounded by the great German Reich. Thus the hostility of Benesch[52] and the French to the annexation. The north-east of Germany however would correspondingly gain in penetrating force. The way to the south could not be shifted any more.

Vienna, Germany's most beautiful city, once the focus of an individual, most attractive German culture, filled with men of insight, energy, and taste - perhaps today still without a hard political will - can, united with the Reich, become that which was once created for it by its European significance: a great postern-gate of German cultural and economic importance towards the south-east. Then the addition of the foreign population will disappear through the new infusion of German blood. Vienna is worth more than a mass. To it is eternally attached the greatness of German cultural influence upwards from the Danube. But also, already, the reverence before his own political, intellectual and economic history alone demands peremptorily from the German that Austria be not given up, that it be annexed to the Reich. The coming Germany should be no large-territorial state predetermined by any princely house however famous. Austria can be given up in the coming Germany as little as old Prussia. The proudest traditions which today must once again be made fruitful are indeed bound to the Austrian special development of the German type.

Moreover, the reunion is a demand of national honour: it is not subject to calculations of usefulness. The short-sighted person sees at best the next day - mostly only the past. Narrowness of heart and mind of the person believing in parties ignores the unconditionality of the national cultural demand. Betrayed by the split understanding and the healthy political feeling, he dreams of being clever, if he - reluctant regarding the diversion from the accustomed internal political field of vision - counts up with a funereal tone the number of Catholics or Jews, of Social Democrats or of "reactionary" Christian-Socialists, which disturbs the most important thing which he gives for the dogged party-follower: the count of a majority. Without success. Their camp, which, already ten

---

52 Edvard Benes (1884-1948) was instrumental in forming the first Czech government in 1918 in which he served as Foreign Minister until 1935. Benes championed the League of Nations and opposed plans for the union between Austria and Germany. He negotiated treaties with Romania and Yugoslavia which formed the Little Entente, which was later in 1924 joined by France and served as a bloc against Germany.

years before, encompassed the majority of the Reich Germans, becomes daily smaller in all parties, it disintegrates. The inferiority of such a way of thought is seen through. Significant for the change also in Austria is the government declaration of the Federal Chancellor, Seipel,[53] on 19 May, 1927, in the Viennese Representative Assembly: "Quite especially in our hearts lies the formation of our relation to our brothers in the German Reich. In an intellectual context, the relation can naturally not become narrower any longer. We are bound to them through the same origin, same cultural development and same history. But we wish, beyond that, to promote everything which can make the approximation of the two states a closer one in the economic or other fields. We shall strive in this way to make progress as much as is possible and permissible according to the state of affairs". In the way of full reunion with the Reich naturally! It is demanded loudly by racial bonds and prepared by quiet, unofficial annexation- and assimilation-work from both sides. It is superfluous here to speak of political, economic, and cultural details.

The liberation of the German border lands, however, and their reunion with the German state, is such a self-evident demand that it does not require a foundation. It is not appropriate to expose it longer to degermanisation than is at all necessary. Large German and border German demands supplement and condition one another.

VIII: The European goals

The future federal politics is basically different from that of the pre-war period. The latter knew only two form-groups: the free federation or the firm states union. Two forms of federation were further in use: the genuine federation between two approximately equally strong states which joined together with equal rights for the common attainment of this or that goal under preservation of their full sovereignty (in the sense of the western conception of the state); then, the treaty between a power and powerless states which had more or less lost their independence. For example: the treaties of the French Revolution government and that of the first Kaiser Reich, England's "federations" in overseas territories with

---

53 Ignaz Seipel (1876-1932) was Federal Chancellor of Austria (1922-24, and again in 1926). Seipel was an opponent of Social Democracy and a critic of the parliamentary system of democracy which he sought to counteract with a strengthening of the Heimwehr. Although he retired from political leadership in 1929, he remained influential in Austrian internal policy until the end of his life.

Indian princes, or those of the American Union with Central American states. If one wished to move closer together one required to enter into indissoluble bonds. Monarchic personal union does not need to be taken into consideration in this connection. Commonality between certain state institutions characterises the state unions, lasting unifications of two or more states for the purpose of uniform or similar exercise of sovereign rights, without needing to consider "the union" and its organs in order to undertake government transactions within the individual states. A still closer bond was the federal state on the nature of which the science set up many mutually divergent doctrines regarding the question of where the sovereignty lies, whether it is divisible, etc. Unconcerned about this conflict, such federal states foreign politically uniformly directed and defended prospered, to be sure not always without inner frictions. Actually it is a matter of whether these structures have arisen from the relaxation of older historical unions (Austria-Hungary) and whether the tendency towards the separation still continued to predominate, or whether related or otherwise, mostly through language-community or blood mixture, closely linked states were in the process of binding themselves to one another still more firmly (the United States of America and Brazil).

All these models do not suit Europe, for it requires a full new formation. Such a one was, however, until now observed among nations of equal origin and language. Multi-national Switzerland looked back, before the Confederation assumed its present form, already to a centuries-old common history. Much less does the model of the Geneva national federation, of a loose state union, suit, in spite of some determinations making dissolution harder, and above all not the new British one of 1926. The British state union has become uniquely historical: bound externally only by the crown, internally however by community of language, by total clogging of British interests, and by the sea-ruling navy. Where the community of language is not perfect, lie the weak points (South Africa). The union of nations, however, brings so many congenital mistakes openly to view that only a superficial observer can plan to "order" Europe according to the model of the union of nations or indeed as that of its subdivision. Rather the internal new structure of Soviet Russia can offer suggestions. For, in many respects, there were there similar tasks to be resolved which arose from the multiplicity of peoples. The difference lies, however, in the fact that the Bolshevist total state, ruling over the entire territory, was at first already present and then split itself up subsequently, for the facilitation of the administration, into partial republics - according to language and race, in order to pre-empt dangers which would have to arise from the dissatisfaction with the uniform tendency towards administration. Nobody forced the power-holders in Moscow to it. They did it out of free pieces, partly from considerations of utility, partly in order to realise old Socialist-Syndicalist doctrines of the earlier age.

Still more differently stand matters in non-Communistic Europe. It decomposes not only into languages and races - in extreme cases awakening races like the Ukrainian -, but into many large and old political peoples: full of marked racial personalities with much famed history and hard outlines, with a peculiar intellectual and economic culture, with a more or less established state system. Next to these we find small- and medium- nations, younger and poorer in tradition, still with so much more reckless nationalism, mostly stuck still deep in their adolescence. Preferred in the conclusion of the Versailles treaty, they unjustly received their own states with all-too broadly drawn borders in which they could rule freely thanks to the victory of the atomistic French national state doctrine, without consideration of the foreign national parts wrongly apportioned to them, of their neighbouring nations, or of the European community. The self-interest of states therefore stands today in full bloom. It produces evil fruits.

The untenability of the European map arisen from 1918 to 1920 is admitted by the public opinion of all nations. To repeat the causes and reasons of this condition would be a waste of space. They are not only of an economic, but also, in high measure, of a political sort. The deficient resolution of the question of nationalities shelters visible dangers. The powerless and chained German people poses to the European politics more of an enigma than earlier the powerful did: an idea which Stegemann has brilliantly developed in his *Illusion of Versailles*.[54] The doctrine of the self-determination right of the peoples directed against the Germans and the Hungarians, once announced in the "Declaration of Lausanne" adopted by Wilson during the world war, is today turned against the artificially inflated would-be victor states. It begins to work in favour of the Germans and Hungarians and destroys the European state picture of the Versailles treaty.

Thus there sounds everywhere the cry for a new order of Europe, to be sure, differently tuned according to the standpoint of the speaker and according to his way of thought: in western Europe, in the better established national states, more cautiously, even if the economics there,

---

54 Hermann Stegemann (1870-1945), *Das Trugbild von Versailles: weltgeschichtliche Zusammenhänge und strategische Perspektiven*, Stuttgart: Deutsche Verlags Anstalt, 1926.

stifled by military burdens and out of fear of America's competition, wishes for real establishment of peace. In the satellite states, most loudly. There the economic self-sufficiency (autarchy) striven for at present was quickly recognized as a chimera, even if until now the state leadership holds fast to it. The scope of these state economies is indeed too small. Larger economic structures seem necessary. All attempts however to re-establish the earlier Habsburg Empire at least as an economic Danube confederation were wrecked on political oppositions. Austria wants it as little as Hungary.

Need then indeed promotes plans to organise Europe, but not the solving formula: what as such was offered as allegedly new, indeed partly was extolled like a trade ware, is old wine in new bottles. Anxiously concerned to maintain the present distribution of power, without really undermining the present day western state - Socialist varnishing does not change its system for the better - all the following mentioned reforms wish however finally only a sham-democratic state federation. The catch-word of equality and freedom are transferred from the internal political to the external political field. One wishes to transform the whole of Europe into a gigantic mass democracy, which raise the lies of the equal and free rule of people into a proportion of immensity.

IX: Ineffective or wrong plans

At first, economic plans were submitted to the public by Socialists, but also by the "capitalistic" side. They recommended almost throughout a European customs union, partly according to the previous private economic union.[55] Esteemed economic unions emphasized in announcements, and at the various conferences, the necessity of the economic "co-operation" of the European states. Traffic conferences wanted to remove Europe's turn-pikes. A manifesto coloured in the free-trade style wanted international financial people to tear up Europe's economy-restricting customs walls. In Geneva, the economics conference, in Paris, the international chamber of commerce, was concerned in the same way.

Others recognized in advance that the European question is

---

55 Paul [Göhre, *Deutschlands weltpolitische Zukunft*, Berlin, Kurt Vorwinkel,] 1925; [August Schmidt, *Das neue Europa*, Berlin, Reimar Hobbing,] 1925; Wladimir [Woytinsky, *Die Vereinigten Staaten von Europa*, Berlin, J.H.W. Dietz Nachfolger Verlag,] 1926.

however not, in the first place, determined by considerations of utility. "To conceive it from this point of view is a way of observation which reminds one of the politics of the pre-war period, in which we expected everything from economic and power political organisation, a standpoint which has led finally to our present-day chaos. Even this attitude betrays a not all-too deep insight into the forces determining the development" (Kleefisch). The historical-Catholic "West" movement seeks therefore to revive once again the universalistic idea of the Holy Roman Empire of German nations. Accordingly, the Austrian prince, Karl Anton von Rohan undertook to bind the conservative ruling class of the European nations with his *Europäische Revue* and through conferences.[56] "For the supplementing of the communication work of the governments" arose further a union for European communication, into which famous politicians entered: Luther, Stresemann, Wirth, Vandevelde, Briand, Painlevé, Albert Thomas, Ramsay MacDonald, Fritjof Nansen, etc. But this union must fail because good words and dispositions are useless; for action, however, this circle is organised in a too motley manner; its forces eliminate one another.

The reach of all these efforts was, and is, small, their powers are modest; they consist at the present of a book and a newspaper or of one or two conferences in the year which give an opportunity for expression. Their objectives are either economic or cultural-intellectual. They do without the comprehensive, pick out only details, without giving firm outlines to that which is demanded. Thus their effectiveness too remained small. Even for the future nothing is to be expected from them but relaxation through criticism.

It is different with the so-called Pan-European movement. It sets in with easily comprehensible recipes which are immediately coined into catch-words, promoted by a charlatanish advertising campaign. Their founder and their driving force is Count Nikolaus von Coudenhove-Kalergi in Vienna.[57] Of his way of thought one gets the following idea in his book on the aristocracy: "The man of the distant future will be a mongrel", so prophesies the son of an already mixed "Austrian" aristocrat and a Japanese woman. "The eurasiatic-negroid future race, externally

56 Prince Karl Anton Rohan (1898-1975) was an Austrian cultural historian who founded, in 1924, the 'Verband für kulturelle Zusammenarbeit' and published, from 1925, the *Europäische Revue*. His books include *Schiksalsstunde Europas* (1937) and *Heimat Europa* (1954).
57 Count Richard Coudenhove-Kalergi (1894-1972), leader of the `Paneuropa' movement, sought to maintain his idea of European unity upto the sixties.

perhaps similar to the ancient Egyptian, will replace the multiplicity of the peoples with a many-sidedness of personality". On the leaders of this future development he says: "Instead of destroying Judaism, it has ennobled Europe against its will through that artificial selection process (steeling through heroically borne martyrdom and purging of weak-willed, intellectually poor elements, of which he has spoken in the earlier sentence) and trained it into a leader nation of the future. No wonder therefore that this people, arisen from the ghetto, develop themselves into an intellectual aristocracy of Europe. Thus a kind providence has, through the grace of the spirit, gifted Europe a new noble race the moment that the feudal nobility fell, through the emancipation of the Jews". To this half-coloured mongrel the concept of race and national culture means nothing for understandable reasons.

In 1923 he published a programme piece *Paneuropa* and won with it European fame, especially in circles which were in advance favourably disposed to him on account of his book on the aristocracy. His introductory statement, "This book is determined to awake a great political movement", he has made true. Externally, Pan-Europe was a success: not alone thanks to propagandistic performances, through its easily comprehensible symbols - the sun-cross as the sign of humanity and reason - and through the timely capitalisation of a need of the time, but also, above all, through its penetrating criticism of the conditions of the present-day Europe.

Its foundation is, of course, wrong; for he says, "The entire European question culminates in the Russian problem. The main goal of the European politics must be the prevention of a Russian invasion ---." "If Russia succeeds, through some harvests, to revive itself economically, before Europe is united - then Europe's fate is sealed. The future state form of Russia is thereby irrelevant. As soon as the opportunity offers itself to Russia to bring Europe into its dependence, it will make use of this possibility - whether it is now red or white". That sets the facts on their head. Soviet Russia is weak in economy and army, apparently for a long time. Certainly, the fact of the disappearance of the predominantly Nordic ruling class in Russia is highly significant for the future. Only the knowledge of this circumstance preserves one from the politics dangerous for Europe of democratising and capitalising Russia. A Pan-Slavism of the nihilistic sort of a Dostoievski would thus grow with a dangerous rise. The western historical conception therefore saw correctly in the Russian field European colonial soil, in the Russian peasant masses men who must be ruled in a European manner. There are, therefore, with regard to Russia, only two political ways of which one is hard to enter: to bring Russia once again under the rule of a European ruling class; the other is marked by the history of the Middle Ages and the battle of Tannenberg in 1914, one of the few which has true world historical significance: to push the European culture towards the East. Later generations will praise the destruction of Russia as the great performance of the German people; as much more tactically correct it may perhaps have been to preserve it at first. It means, however, to ignore the present-day situation of Europe, if one does not perceive in the forcing back of the Russian Empire one of the great possibilities for the German foreign policy. From a broad perspective therefore partial consent could be granted to the thought processes of the Pan-European Count if he advocates a truly European policy against Russia. Never, however, can such be conducted if the emphasis of Europe lies in the west. A French anti-Russia politics must always treat Germany and central Europe as an intermediate territory. In fact, however, the emphasis of European self-maintenance lies in the European centre, in Prussia. Without this even the Rhine and, therewith, France are lost.

Coudenhove acknowledges the Paris peace treaties, which signify to him, in spite of his criticism, "politically a progress in comparison to the pre-war situation". He glosses over its consequences: "As unjust and damnable also as these suppressions of parts (Germans, Magyars, and Ukrainians) are: to these suppressed peoples of today at least there remains their own state as a national resort and as a free cultural centre - whereas, before the war, European cultured nations were in their entirety robbed of their national freedom. In spite of this remnant of national suppression, for the removal of which every good European must work, a progress is accordingly to be recognized in the political structure of Europe of the pre-war period". For this reason, the much-mixed Count also teaches the irrevocability of the borders drawn in Paris; for this reason, too, his hostility to annexation: one who works for a change of the German borders must conduct war politics. Thereby did Vilna come without a war to Poland, Oedenburg to Hungary! The Belgian cabinet decided in 1926 to sell Eupen-Malmedy to the Reich. If this decision too was repealed once again on Poincaré's[58] insistence, it still shows the

---

58 Raymond Poincaré (1860-1934) was President of the Third Republic (1913-20) and Premier of France, from 1926. Belgium was prepared by 1926 to transfer Eupen-Malmedy to Germany in order to alleviate its fiscal problems by redeeming the German "occupation marks" in Belgium at an advantageous value. However, when Poincaré was appointed Premier, he opposed all territorial changes, and the projected transfer came to nought.

erroneousness of Coudenhove's thesis that one must make the best of the Versailles drawing of borders: "One who attacks these borders - attacks the peace of Europe".

Coudenhove's plans have perceptibly experienced extensive rejection in serious political circles. Even from national German parties, whose thought arose from the same individualistic root, the following was smaller than the criticism. Even leftist circles in the Reich rejected Coudenhove because his doctrine takes as its point of departure the work of the Paris treaty and makes the hegemony of France the chief column of his system. Nevertheless, Coudenhove found for years his chief support among the Berlin bank circles, while one overlooked in France what useful assisting peoples the pan-Europeans could become for the guarantee of the things acquired in the work of the Paris treaty. Finally, however, the French foreign minister, Briand,[59] explained in the summer of 1929 in a commission of the French chamber that he would submit plans for the "United States of Europe" to the powers in the autumn; Coudenhove approved Briand's plan in a public announcement.[60] Now the connection is clearly established.

The foundation of Coudenhove is the individualistic national state with its formal democracy. He instructed in 1923: "Europe as a political concept encompasses all democratic and semi-democratic states of continental Europe with the inclusion of Iceland --- The remaining territory of European Turkey belongs politically to Asia". The Europe to be founded by Coudenhove "reaches so far to the east as the democratic system; the question whether Russia belongs to Europe the Count sees as "made essentially simple" since it has placed itself outside Europe through its break with the democratic system. "The addition of England and Ireland to Pan-Europe would be possible after the disintegration of the British world empire".

Pan-Europe should thus consist of 26 larger and 7 smaller territories with 300,000,000 inhabitants. In addition even the overseas colonial empire of the Pan-European powers enter with 53,000 inhabitants in Africa and 78,300,000 inhabitants in other continents. - What is such a

---

59 Aristide Briand (1862-1932) served eleven times as Premier of France. In 1926 he was awarded the Nobel Peace Prize (which he shared with Gustav Stresemann) for his contributions towards international cooperation and the League of Nations.
60 See Richard Coudenhove-Kalergi, *Paneuropa, 1922 bis 1966*, Wien: Verlag Herold, pp.64-66; *History of the Paneuropean Movement*, Basle and Vienna: Paneuropa Union, 1962, p.10f.

union of states with 431 million inhabitants? Super-imperialistic formal democracy with all the mistakes of the past, a product of megalomaniac intoxication of numbers!

Coundenhove's strict advance limitation of the future union of European states, which he later sought to moderate somewhat, ignores the territory. Already for this reason it is superficial and false. If forms, however, the essential factor of his individualistic thought "in states". In addition, it is, because cumbersome, awkward. Western way of thought in a pacifist variety conducted to the highest degree, already almost to a caricature, robs the European construction plans in advance of every freedom of movement, what Coudenhove moreover does not overlook entirely. Dull and uncreative, but for that reason easily understandable to like-minded people, Coudenhove knows only states and state nations but not peoples, not driving cultural movements. To want to prescribe firm borders means to ignore that Europe is, historically, intellectually- and religiously, communications politically, and economically, only a very conditional unity. For, towards the borders it increasingly evaporates.

Popular feeling and nationalistic chauvinism are however the same thing for Coudenhove. For that reason, the secrets of this earth, as openly as they may lie, must remain hidden to the Pan-European. He does not wish to see them. The one robbed of the idea of the whole is made a fool of by his belief in the understanding. He fails before simple facts, such as those of the westerner in general.

Europe is not to be built up once again from the rubble of the destruction with construction plans out of individualistic-pacifist thought. Not the fear of Soviet Russia, but the concern about the unresolved pains of the people which break up the ground for Bolshevist seed, must be the mainspring of all work towards a new legal order. Finally: no true architect builds from outside inwards. That only those who are not experts do. Such constructions suffice for film shooting.

If the Pan-Europeans work with cosmopolitan-pacifistic means in order to give Europe a new face, Fascism does with the opposite. Already above - in the internal political part - serious doubts were brought forward, whether Fascism does not represent a culmination of nationalistic-imperialistic intellectual tradition, and therefore has remained even in that Liberalism which it allegedly strives to overcome. This book evaluates its internal political performance (deliberate economic politics, national education, constitutional reform) even as highly as its effort to set a penetrating intellectual doctrine against the western democracy. But the Fascist state centralism has, until now, as little got around to the hurdles of the creation of a ranked society as it has not succeeded, on the other hand, to sketch a picture of the correct coming European order. The Italian politics in South Tyrol strengthens the doubt that Fascism until now has remained in a radicalisation of the national-political idea.

This process is not new. Even the German Liberalism fell already decades ago into political-national radicalism. Every genuine revolution, however, brings not merely a change of methods but the removal of the ruling principle. Thus the individual was perhaps dethroned in Italy, but even the personality destroyed. Precisely in this way the foreign policy of the deceptive pacifism was removed, but the racial personality too was destroyed. Fascism has not yet, until now, accomplished the turn towards organic life. The incorporation into a final unconditional worth, which the whole of life constantly offers to man, is lacking. The tendency of the West to anarchy was thereby only externally chained by Fascism, but not combated from inside.

X: The foundations of German federal politics

The correct way is the reverse. One should begin from inside. No new construction can do without the core, which it has to let grow gradually. In this way do crystals also arise. The cell must lie in the field of the greatest difficulties, political and economic: there, where the treaties of the Paris suburbs tore up the finest inter-weavings, where the European peoples and states pushed against one another without natural borders, where the closed settlement territory of the peoples were recently sliced politically and where peoples are crowded in such a mixed situation that state borders can in general not be drawn on the basis of national segregation. The core territory, on the needs of which the legal decrees of a union of European states must be torn apart, lies not at the border of Europe, either in the north or in the west, nor even in the extreme east, but in the centre, which has no geographically limited territory: in the territory of the settlement field of the German, and of the east- and south-European medium and lesser peoples, from the Baltic Sea to the Adriatic, from Finland to the Aegean and the Black Sea.

This territory is central Europe, enlarged by the near south-eastern Europe and the near eastern Europe, that which Albrecht Haushofer[61] called Inner Europe. A presentation of this territory and of the foundations of essential federal formation is given by Karl C. von

---

61 [September, 1926, issue of the *Volk und Reich*, Berlin.]

Loesch.[62] Premature inclusion of the border territories of Europe makes the problem more difficult and blurs the goal.

A cell must be present to which states and peoples can be joined economically and politically. The greatest unity of this territory is the German people, the greatest of its states is the torso of the German Reich. Thence the duty and right of the Germans to the leadership in a European new formation. This conception is to be founded also economic historically, not only in remembrance of the Prussian customs-union. For, the greatest part of the territory just mentioned has received in the last 1000 years not only its intellectual but also its economic culture from Germans or through German transmission. German is there the language of trade and large communications, the work methods of the economy are German. Germans have been living there for centuries in larger and smaller islands as soil-related as the other peoples: economically a model, as a mediator unsurpassable.

The closed central European settlement territory of the Germans however reaches from the North Sea to the Baltic Sea (upto 70km. as the crow flies) almost to the Adriatic. The intermediate sector is little passable, chalk formations and foothills of the Alps fill it. Precisely there lives one of the smallest peoples of Europe. Bays of the ocean still reach even into German land. Almost all transport ways from east to west and from south to north, on land and by air, lead over the territory of the Germans: thus these are actually Europe's people of the centre. Thus, almost without natural borders or limits, Germany is politically and militarily threatened or favoured: exposed to attacks and prepared for attack.

Italic, Italian-Germanic, Germanic, and Slavic peoples, and further a people belonging to a special group, border on the German: the picture of the neighbours is therefore more mottled than anywhere else.

According to its blood mixture, the German is also in a central situation. The Nordic blood, extirpated in Russia, fully attenuated in the west and the south, predominant in the north and in the Netherlands but fully subjected to individualism in terms of the intellect and will, is still sufficiently present in Germany.

The German people must once again become legal creative, in order to find new political ideas for itself and Europe: in order to facilitate a living together of peoples on the same territory, in a painful narrowness. Beginnings towards this are already present in many fields. It is important

---

62 ["Paneuropa - Völker und Staaten", in *Staat und Volkstum*, Berlin, Deutscher Schutzbund Verlag], 1926.

to give them shape in order to provide, in this way, to the foreign policy of the Reich, intellectual weapons which are more effective than those until now. Only in this way can the repeatedly characterised tendency against the European centre which leads away from the German culture be reversed into an opposite movement which leads to the collection of the people in the centre of Europe. The foundation of a universally valid European order is, accordingly, dependent on the Germans returning once again to their basic ideas of truth and justice and clothing them in modern decrees. The people which tramples underfoot the humanitarian lie of Europe and hoists the flag of true order becomes the self-active head of the new European organism. The loss of the ability "to highlight the European aspect of the German people" (Karl Anton, Prince Rohan) was responsible for the divergence of Europe from the people of the centre. The historical hour requires the full setting in of the German people for the European new formation under total affirmation and strengthening of its powers derived from the spirit of the people.

In the national political part, the picture of the coming German state was already sketched, whose forms facilitate a politics of firm federation. Since the economy, separated from the political in a certain sense, can follow its own laws, but the federation politics projected here extends the nourishment territory, the stimulus for imperialistic economic politics ceases. The same is true of the cultural life. Therewith the striven-for federation politics of the new individualistic (organic) state and of the impulse towards extension lying within it lost its threatening, or indeed hostile, aspect for the neighbouring peoples which clung inseparably to the individualistic-national state foreign politics. However, a state of the western sort, which emerged economically and culturally imperialistically, had to push the adjoining border peoples. The new Germany, however, from whose realm of influence culture and economy are derived, needs to instil no fear any longer into border peoples who rightly wish the fruits of their own work and their racial character to be untouched. Such a state exerts an attractive influence on its neighbours. For, it offers to smaller people through new federal forms the powerful attraction of being able to participate in the advantages of a superior culture, of a developed economy, without having to give themselves up. Thus arises a healthy federal foundation whereas the all-consuming, all-ruling state was disposed of. A state system constituted in this way can offer a secure dwelling place even to a foreign people who stand racially, geopolitically, culturally or historically close to the Germans.

Now what differentiates in the final analysis the Italian concept of the national state from the new political idea which should replace it? What makes it really capable of introducing a new European order? On the one hand, the legal idea which recognizes the rights of other peoples; on the other hand, the greater flexibility. Deep love for one's own people leads, through the knowledge that in every people a higher personality is embodied, even with necessity to the attention to foreign peoples and to the striving for a higher legal order among the peoples. To develop and demarcate independent laws of the racial personality with regard to the whole that is sought is a part of the new German foreign political goal. Hereby, however, it does not occur without border changes; the latter, however, have as a pre-requirement a far-reaching change of the spiritual basic attitude of the Europeans, the change of the state conceptions in general. Since a new legal order has as a pre-requirement the demarcation of rights, ordering principles must be set up. Karl C. von Loesch[63] has outlined them as follows:

"1. Every people should have in future the right to maintain its racial existence and to develop itself freely. The only limitation which is necessary - just as the right of the individual man in the state must be limited in favour of the maintenance of the whole - occurs to the benefit of an ordered living together of the peoples: from the "rights of the peoples" therefore follow also "duties of the peoples".

2. As political basic rights of the peoples the following are to be considered:

for the closed settlement territory of every people[64] the right to their own state.

for the sections of the people not comprehended by this, which remain outside and live in foreign states as their citizens, the right to maintenance of the intellectual and physical racial existence (racial group right)."

The recognition of the right to one's own state does not naturally signify, for the peoples coming into question, the pressure towards the severing of the existing historical, territorial, and economic bonds (between peoples who live on the edge of the closed settlement territory in an interconnection of peoples or in a racial mixture in language islands or mixed-language territories); much less the prohibition of a far-reaching

---

63 [October issue, 1928, of the *Deutsche Rundschau*], pp.1-21, "Streben und Stil der Besiegten: Außenpolitischen Überlegungen für das deutsche Volk".

64 [The establishment of the closed racial territory will often not be easy. Wide territories of Europe are debated. The application of mechanical principles for the establishment of the range of a nation is prohibited by itself. Popular votes do not come into consideration in all cases, often indeed the pre-war population was driven away by force.]

voluntary association. Pressure in no form comes into question here; it is a matter, however, of avoiding pressure. The will of the peoples is the decisive thing. What a people is is, today, to be sure, still in no way firm; so many racial sections are claimed by two, indeed three, peoples precisely in the most dangerous storm-centres of Europe. Nevertheless, in practice, useful guidelines are easily to be found if only one avoid unfruitful historicism (historical proof) and the beloved equation of language community and racial membership.

If, however, greater parts of racial bodies remain bound to foreign peoples, the degree of rights which suits them depends on the numerical relation, on the manner of settlement, on their historical and cultural significance for the whole of the state; whether they are authorized to demand recognition as a people of the state with equal rights or whether guaranteed racial group rights (autonomy) suffice, which also will have different scopes. Decisive are the absolute and relative number of a racial group, the density of their population, and the manner of their settlement, their social significance, their economic and communication-technological connections, their cultural development, their historical traditions, and their traditional attitude to the state-administering people. The right of free and equal use of their own language and to all possibilities which the public life offers, as well as the right to maintenance, care, and development of their own racial culture according to the principles of the public-legal corporate body autonomy forms the indispensable pre-requirement for each people. In any case, the ordering of this question must result in the form of constitutional determinations which cannot be changed by majority decisions".

That is, however, only one side of the problem, which requires supplementation. "Along with the right of the peoples to their own, even characteristic, political existence (racial group rights are also such partial rights which are opposed by the wrong conception of the system of the state ruling today, which does not wish to recognize the other spheres of rights) a binding link is to be set up as the fusion of the impulse to uniformity and the tendency to isolation. The consideration of one's neighbours and the closer relations produced by the neighbourliness demand an establishment of neighbourly rights and duties of the states.[65]

---

65 [The rights and duties of the peoples in the state and of the states as neighbours condition one another reciprocally. They must, harmonized to and among one another, be built up. Border changes, as they are inevitable for a true satisfaction, can be carried out for themselves alone without dangerous conflicts only with difficulty. Neighbourly approximation without border changes stand at the

Wars are kindled, according to experience, mostly through neighbourly friction. To avoid them is the first pre-requirement for the removal of the feeling of the uncertainty under which the states suffer today. This closer binding of the neighbours forms at the same time the indispensable preliminary stage for the progressing towards the organic structure, the building up of greater economic territories which are indeed necessary if Europe wishes to maintain itself in the competition of the continent. That does not, however, mean, by far, recommending mechanical equalisation of the states and rash bindings of the states, for which the time has not yet become ripe. On the contrary! As regards neighbourly bindings of the states of the same territory, the development must rather rise gradually in organic growth from inside outwards for the formation of higher federalistic unities".

The idea of a federation, as it is expressed here, starts even from the fact that the society consists of partial realms, that it itself already divides out intellectual circles of life of a special sort and performance. Walter Heinrich[66] says on this, that the state of such a conception appears as that order (*status*) which lends to every society historical shape and form. Since every racial section, every racial fragment and every people strives to bring its life into form, within every people its life must be shaped systematically: its artistic, economic, original and familial life-expressions. "All these life expressions must be collected in a strong protecting cover, in an order which, accomplishes those foreign and internal political performances which we have characterised as state performances. There are naturally different degrees of development of this political life. Political life is a concept of degree[67] (not only, as a typographical mistake will have it, a basic concept[68]). Not every people or indeed every racial section can develop its own political life which could be designated as a racial full state. That seems also thoroughly comprehensible. For, for an organic historical stratum, which is the true one, nowhere can an equality of peoples be established, but one observes always and everywhere the greatest inequality, in the fullness of being of

---

moment on account of the justified resentment of those who suffer injustice today against other psychological hindrances. The basic agreement is still lacking from which first a European feeling can grow which is the pre-requirement of lasting and stable associations. Both goals cannot be reached in one stroke. More or less numerous objective and territorial interim solutions will have to precede them.]
66 [July issue of the *Europäische Revue*, 1929.]
67 'Gradbegriff'.
68 'Grundbegriff'.

the peoples as well as in their historical tasks and their historical significance. Sociological and historical research finds everywhere and always the tendency of every culture and every racial section to develop the political life suited to its being. This political life can manifest very different degrees of development and even does manifest them; this ladder proceeds from the most primitive beginnings of a kernel political life (e.g. in the form of a hardly performed autonomy, hardly present closedness with regard to other peoples of the state, and hardly traceable bindings to other peoples, perhaps to the entire nation, of which the concerned racial group is a partial population or "minority") to the fully developed political life which gets perhaps the leading role in foreign and internal politics in their state. All life in society and history strives for political forms and also develops actual political existence).

The organic state is not forced to destroy all that structure of orders which brings life with it. Rather, it may maintain, strengthen and try to develop the intermediate members of the orders. In this way also an organic European state federation can let the individual peoples live. "The more vital and genuine their own life is developed, the stronger and more powerful does the whole appear," says Walter Heinrich of the state: the same is true even of a healthy state binding. Just as the state in reality is not based on the counting together of the wills of the individuals, not on the unorganised randomly flowing masses of state citizens, but on characteristic realms of life, with regard to which it similarly embodies a closed realm of life and performance, namely as the order of political existence, as external and internal concentration, so a European state federation arches over the individual states and peoples naturally under the preservation of their rights with regard to the whole. If there is, in the organic state, already a large number of partial political existences which are endowed with their own life and certain sovereign rights (genuine autonomy), then there arises even through the European federation one more new realm of life. Just as the autonomy of the professional realms is finally not derived (delegated) from the state, but comes also from itself, from the life and objective demands of the whole, so also the European union as a community of the Western peoples and cultures of this continent derives its justification from the living whole. Its realm of tasks is developed as a result of the new ordering of Europe also quite naturally through customs- and economic settlements to the highest development and administration of rights in this realm. It will gradually progress.

It was characteristic for the individualistic state that, as a result of the rigidity of its conceptions, it was not in a position to resolve such a simple problem as, for example, the Catalanian, in a satisfactory manner, because it just cannot acknowledge life realms with their rootedness. It can make no minority forces useful for itself by building them up, because every such attempt (that is the horrible phantom of the individualistic state leaders) would immediately lead to the formation of a "state within a state", and therewith to the destruction of the idol of uniformity. The idea of the organic state, on the other hand, allows greater freedom internally and formative possibilities externally. But centralism is finally nothing but a theory. The German Reich, England, Switzerland and many other states have long demonstrated that states can be capacitated to great performances which bear a federal political or, indeed, a political federation character and thereby permit, under the guarantee of greater mobility, yet a very strict concentration through the highest authority. *Even because this system is so mobile, because it is not sworn to anything, it corresponds best to the varied facts of Europe.* What people are led in an organically built up multi-national state union is finally a historical decision; they can be diverse according to the period, just as in the multi-national states locally diverse solutions are thinkable which do not always summon the numerically greatest people to the leadership. Not every people and not every racial group can attain political maturity. "On this point decide their intellectual, economic, and political powers, finally their historical fate, indeed even the entire nation to which this racial group belong" (Walter Heinrich).

Thus the German people, if it brings forward the power for the European performance, can proclaim the rule of the superior at the same time internal- and foreign-politically. As the pioneers of a higher morality the Germans then become the prophets of a better Europe which can once again gift something to the world and which renews its intellectual predominance. The people of the highest achievement should on the basis of their achievement, under full consideration of its geopolitical central situation, be the leader in a union of free peoples. This leadership will form new spheres of power and culture.

It was a contradiction that small and medium peoples standing first on the threshold of the Western civilisation, for the most part, necessarily doing without an independent culture on account of the too small number of people, could increase the sphere of their power in the last decade under the sign of the idea of the individualistic national state, whereas, at the same time, historical peoples like the German were curtailed and enslaved. It is a sign of the downfall. Only the suppression of genuine culture and the worship of the idol of civilisation can lead to such foolishness. For, where civilisation in its fleetingness and emptiness of content begins to displace the feeling for culture, every difference is blurred: the smallest barbaric race raises its head with civilisatory gestures and demands equal rights. But just as an organic social life is possible only when the rights of the parts, which the member proves to the whole, are ranked according to performances, so also a European order only when right and service are brought into an appropriate relation. There is no naturally given right to life of a people, but only a justification of their existence on the basis of self-felt and self-willed life obligations. The principle of equality, ruling in the self-determination rights of a Wilson, and therefore powerless for a new ordering, was responsible for Europe's anarchy. Even in the field of national relations the path towards genuine worthiness begins to become free once again only with the knowledge of the inequality of nations. For, no order is possible without a series of values, and no justice where formal equality would rule.

Chapter IV

Alfred Rosenberg

"Germany and the League of Nations", *Völkischer Beobachter*, 30 August, 1923.[69]

In the last days the entire so-called German press has been assiduously concerned to represent to us the entry into the League of Nations as an undertaking worth striving for. Even those papers which until now acted with some criticism of this union implore in the sweetest tones and request the masters in Geneva on their knees for admission. It is hard for the average German and not only him to really understand the true essence of this institution. He reads only the speeches of the one or the other representative and believes that the spoken words had the significance which he attributes to them in his good-naturedness.

The *Jüdische Rundschau* wrote in 1920 (No.49): "An English statesman said at a mass-meeting in London that the only two events which could expiate something with the war were the Jewish homeland and the League of Nations. He thereby said something which must awaken the strongest echo in all of us. The realization of Zionism is in the final analysis not possible without the actualisation of the League of Nations". This candid tone from the Jewish-national camp already pointed to quite definite backgrounds which then also were observed at the same time at the opening of the League of Nations. When at that time

---

69 Reprinted in A. Rosenberg, *Kampf um die Macht*, pp.246-249.

the general secretary of the League of Nations went to Geneva, in order to organize its celebratory opening, his first step was a visit to - the grand Rabbi of Geneva, Ginsburger. During this audience the master held a long speech which was happily reproduced by the entire Jewish press. He said among other things that he and his co-workers would "unite on the defence of the Jews, and he cherishes the firm confidence that the League of Nations would fulfil its duty with regard to the Jews. He hopes that the entire Jewry would soon enjoy all human and civic rights. From now on the Jews would no longer appeal in vain to the justice of mankind (*Der Israelit*, November 1920).

When Germany protested against the forcible separation of Eupen-Malmédy, it found deaf ears in the just "League of Nations". It was therewith occupied with caring for the destruction of German culture in West Prussia and Upper Silesia. When Germany set forth guards one after the other against the black outrage in the Rhineland, the humane brothers in Geneva believed that the violation of German women, girls and boys belonged to the present-day world-order.

If we now ask with regard to these facts what a German entry into this international consortium would mean, the answer to this question cannot be doubtful: an entry into the League of Nations would mean the recognition, the recognition confirmed by signature, of the international dictatorship of the stock-exchange, Germany would through this new subjugation designate itself as a slave-colony and welcome a delegate of the Hebrew consortium as the unrestricted master and commander. The great German people would go the same way as Austria has already gone. It would be possible that the German mark would rise at the stock-exchanges, it would be possible that the corn-exchanges of New York would throw a few crumbs to the German slave-people, but a signing of the new decree would only increase the depravity of certain circles of Germany; the growing feeling for honour and freedom would be attempted to be silenced with references to the new success, and there would come once again a time of the worst national demoralisation and grovelling which the coming end still would not yet hinder, but we would find ourselves in a far worse situation than is today itself the case.

It is a world-political witticism that an exchange, which in its entire foundation and activity represents nothing more than a contempt of all human- and national rights, has struck its dwelling in a country which has always been considered as a refuge of the suppressed and persecuted. One must see also in the free Switzerland that the recognition of the present-day League of Nations means nothing more and nothing less than the recognition of the Jewish financial dictatorship over the whole world. How far the matters have already flourished in the present-day

Switzerland we saw two months ago. On June 15, the *Israelitische Wochenblatt für die Schweiz* demanded the prohibition of the sale of the well-known book of Henry Ford, *Der internationale Jude*. On June 23, already the Swiss federal railways issued a decree according to which the mentioned work may not be displayed any longer in the railway book-shops.

Every European state which would like to secure its self-determination in the future must set itself in contradiction to this federation, whose goal is only to set informers in all political and economic circles of all countries in order to be able in this way to incite, as a laughing third, nation against nation, state against state. Behind the corridors of the present-day Hebrew League of Nations the knots are tied to a world-conflict. Into this cruel game Germany is supposed to be led in as a will-less object. If the German people has still in general a life-will, it must defend itself with all its powers against these most recent attempts to delivering it.

From the governments nothing is to be expected.

"Jewish world politics", *Der Weltkampf*, June 1924.[70]

> Now comes the age of great wars and revolutions.
> From them will emerge as victor the international Jewish bank.
> Dostoievski.

Not only individual men but also peoples find their personal life-form only after many false paths. Wars and revolutions signify the signposts on which the changes in the inner spiritual attitude are to be read. We live today in one of the greatest ages of intellectual, political and economic transformations, that is, all peoples of the white race, although some seem still to slumber fully. The catastrophes which have been effected since 1914 and the throes still to come in world-political events are therefore so powerful because never before have the two old polar oppositions between the racial ideas and international world-view lain in such a strong, instinctive, but at the same time conscious, battle as today.

Considered from the political side, it stands beyond doubt that the longing for a closed national state was a definite component in the life of the European peoples forming themselves. In earlier youth this natural instinct was interwoven with the idea of the Roman world-empire, in

---

70 Reprinted in *Kampf um die Macht*, pp.277-296.

which "the sun never set". Later this political will sought refuge in the self-centredness of individual kings and emperors, in the 19th century the economic self-centredness came upon its rule under the sign of the age of the machine.

In France and England, we first see the powers for the construction of a national state consciously at work. The will to uniformity of the French kings prepared the power-political, then also the cultural- and national-political direction of France. Its island situation enabled England to carry out the merging of Saxons and Normans so far as to create the far-reaching uniform British type. From the will to power and racial feeling arose the two great empires and then reached for their part into the destiny of other countries, in which the racial-national discussions had not yet been thought through to clarity: to Germany and Italy. These invasions along with the political counter-reformation gave Germany the possibility only in the 19th century of creating the first preconditions for a racial state. It was similar in Italy. But before this political idea, which strives forth only today under the sign of the chaos and a collapse that has never been before, could emerge into full daylight, there lay, like dough, over Europe a new doctrine: Marxism and economic subjectivism.

Many politicians still conducting themselves in old ways of thought will designate it as erroneous to name "anti-capitalistic" Marxism and capitalistic democracy in one breath, yet every deeper glimpse reveals that both phenomena represent in terms of world-view the same thing, and form the residue of the age of financial rule.

The 19th century brought along with the march of the idea of the national state also the fulfilment of the instinct for expansion of the white race. This will to exploration and conquest had driven the Europeans forwards over oceans and continents to the highest mountains, to the North and South Poles, into the hottest deserts of Africa and Asia. Its mind invented instruments which supplied it the picture of the universe. Indefatigably, rational ideas touched as feelers the secret depths of Nature, to transform with progressing knowledge their hostile forces into powers which became serviceable to man until, finally, invisible waves supplied ideas beyond the globe and man raised himself into the air on wings. World-conquest, that, along with organic occlusion, was the longing of the last five hundred years of European history more than ever before. One nation after the other is settled in distant parts of the world, one factory, one colony arises after the other, with progressing technology this world-state system increasingly binds itself together: giant cruisers, armed fleets, protect, secure and expand this property. "The few trees, not my own, spoil my world-possession", this remark of the ruling hundred-year old Faust was the leading saying which developed at the end of the 19th century to its fulfilment, whose resonances we are experiencing today: discover, conquer, rule the world, the world-rule idea of the white race.

This world-imperialism has many forms: it was active inventively, militarily, technologically and capitalistically. These parts which were at the beginning closely united to the work, fragmented themselves increasingly later: statesman and conquering businessman, scientist and leader of battles, entered almost entirely without connection. And within the organisation there developed in the exploitation, from century to century, a form of devilish world-subjection: the middle-man system, the stock-exchange. In Amsterdam, in London and Paris, there arose those cells of the present-day financial- and world-rule, which, not acting in a way that participated in the powerful drama of a world-conquest but in one that exploited this, became a real post of command of world-politics. Nothing characterizes more the open decay of a world-age than that the former discoverers, conquerors, in short, the masters, withdrew and made place to the middle-man, the businessman and the servant. The way passes from the individual conqueror through the dynastic power-state collected together to the plutocratic parliamentary democracy. In place of the idea of political and religious power entered the worship of wares, of trade and of economic speculation.

Just as the individual man would gladly like to defend an activity really alien to his being with a "world-view", so did even the whole of Europe do this, when in 1789 in Paris a state apparatus become decayed was struck down. In the name of freedom, of fraternity, and of humanity, the golden calf was raised to a God, and in the sign of democracy, that is, of "the rule of the people", began an exploitation of the best racial powers of Europe such as had never existed before. The crude age of the machine - which the prescient Goethe feared, because it will "come and strike" - set in. This age created the megalopolis, the factory strongholds. A generation damned by an unholy fate slaved beneath the earth in coal-shafts, in dirty corners of the cities. Generations alienated from Nature grew up robbed of light and air. They felt no sense and saw no goal in their work, they understood nothing of the nature of production which was provided by work, at which they had rotated the very same piece year in and year out. They conceived of their work as only a mechanical activity which secured them their little bit of life. The originally healthy bond between cause and effect, of judgement on appropriateness and inappropriateness of a regulation, such as the peasant and handicraftsman grown up in Nature exercises, increasingly atrophied. From this mood arose a gloomy revolt justified in the deepest recesses of one's inner personality against destiny, the battle of a stratum of society betrayed of its life-rights which had more or less nothing to lose.

It was quite natural that precisely in the gloomy, seething masses over-excited "world-ideas" took root. A knowledge which does not extend beyond the most immediate circle of influence leaps over with agility all intermediate members and is ready to believe in a distant goal, whether the latter be reachable or only a gleaming will-o'-the-wisp. And, as in the harbour-cities of the world, the sparkling rooms of the pleasure-houses appear to the intoxicated sailor to be royal castles, so there arose before the eyes of a seeking army of millions of workers the idea of international Communism. A mass which could have no idea of the worth of personality let itself be gifted with the "ideal" of a depersonalised world and did not know that this was only a gleaming, empty, phantom. The present age, when one believes to be able to grasp at it, signified the hour of most bitter disillusionment and scepticism. This hour decides on whether that scepticism strikes a world down in ruins or whether from the mad-house of Marxism a way to freedom may still be found.

It signifies an unparalleled tragedy that, in the middle of the 19th century, for the armies of striving workers no greater representative arose who, rooted with all his veins in his culture, had through his personality bound past and present in order to gift to the millions a world-view for the future. But in the place of such a representative an incomprehensible fate brought forth two Jews: Marx and Lassalle. The occasion of giving a religious content to the justified workers' movement conducting the battle for bare existence was missed. The Romantic Socialism of a Weitling was not deepened but falsified into a plutocratic Marxism.

What Marx's fanatical personality brought was essentially the same world-view which precisely those people paid homage to against whom the battle of the workers was directed or had to be directed: the lords in the banks and, in the stock-exchange, so many industrial upstarts. The "expropriation of the expropriators" is, in the final analysis, the beginning and end of the Marxist disintegration of the people. Instead of favoring the workers with a new idea, Marx stole the "world-view" of the practical materialist. Instead of preaching a religious, freeing ideal to the enslaved, he threw a flat, Darwinistic, empty world-view rubbish at his feet. Instead of setting up for him as a goal a real homeland and the striving for a national culture, he increasingly freed him inwardly from his fathers, taught him to hate the history of his people and believe in a nebulous "international". This poisonous seed of hatred against one's own people has perhaps been the greatest crime of Marxism against all nations. From it follow the others with necessity.

The "world-view" bases of democracy are therefore the same. They were worked out partly from the spirits of an age of decline, partly set forth, perfected, and propagated by the Jews hostile to everything European. As the "plastic demon of the disintegration of mankind" (Richard Wagner), the Hebrew emerged since that time in the plutocratic, as well as in the allegedly anti-capitalistic Marxist camp. These two facts: the Jewish leadership and the flat, materialistic world-view make it clear why the limitless private capitalism has always conducted itself so well with the "communistic" Social Democracy, works together with it even today and even in the future will make common political and economic businesses so long as it still represents a force.

The international idea demands necessarily a leading point of all questions. Politically this ideal is called a world-republic, economically a world-bank, cultural-politically it is expressed for example in the Esperanto, established by the Jewish Zamenhof,[71] in the rootless Futurism, in the modern Negro music of our metropolises.

In January 1922, the Jew, Walter Rathenau, stood as the "representative of the international financial spirit" and uncrowned ruler of the German Republic from November 1918 before the conference participants at Cannes. He said at the end of his long reparation speech: "The way to which one wishes to devote oneself seems to me correct: an international syndicate, and indeed a private syndicate". Today we stand in the midst of this development towards the all-Jewish private syndicate. But not only because for a few years we confront this warmly wished-for goal of international financial politics, but the world war was one of the means of accelerating this development to economic enslavement of all the nations. Well-known today in German circles is another statement of the same Rathenau, that the time has come when the emperors and kings have to relinquish their place to the financial lords. This statement was written in 1912, thus two years before the outbreak of the world catastrophe. "War is an enormous business undertaking, whereby not the heroism of the soldiers but the business organisation is the finest thing, and America is proud of the favorable business situation which it experiences". In this way does the American Jew Isaac Markussohn triumph in 1917 at a festival in Rotterdam (*The Times*, 3 March 1917).

In London - as well as in Paris and Vienna - for a long time already, the Rothschilds have been ruling. And, thereafter, the children of Israel have, as if by a natural law, emerged increasingly into the foreground of the world-political events.

As if by a natural law! For, every history is finally racial history.

---

71 Ludovic Lazaraus Zamenhof (1859-1917) was a Polish physician and philologist who published his *Lingvo Internacia* in 1887.

Race cannot be explained from the environment, for there will always remain an irresoluble remainder which is not to be resolved either by the climate nor by soil-constitution, nor by adaptation. If the European races brought along with them as essential character-traits the conquering instinct, the inventive, creative mind, the Jewry embodies the commercial, pure speculative, uncreative. "A nation of businessmen and cheaters" did Kant call the Hebrews who already today peddle his name for themselves. Therefore we see the Jews, according to their complete racial inbreeding, at once attracted as by a magnet to settle in trade places and caravan centres. Already long before the powerful "diaspora" through Titus, they were divided over the entire world known at that time, even so assiduously as today active in a speculating, money-lending, brokerish way.

The Jewish colony in Rome is already mentioned in 139 B.C. It had settled there on the shore of the Tiber where the Phoenician and Greek businessmen offered their wares. There also did they remain, and neither flooding nor sicknesses drove the Jews from this place. Only when other places of exchange and trade - as for example in royal castles - appeared more advantageous did they move. So was it everywhere: in Spain, Portugal, France, Italy, Germany and England.

The democratic ideas of the French Revolution, from which the race-destroying parliamentarism arose, falsified the ideal of the national state that was becoming increasingly stronger; together with the growth of the stock-exchange system, they made it possible also in this age of the transition from conqueror to tradesman for the Jewry to exert fully its primal instincts once again. As a born intermediary, therefore, appears - as mentioned before, with natural necessity - the Jewish banker in all the centres of Europe. He possesses the rights of the state in which he lives but pays homage at the same time to his own religious-political-racial religion of law, and primal blood-bonds bound the bankers of Paris, Berlin, and London. The business principle of the House of Rothschild has from the beginning been to never strike a great stock-exchange blow without earlier having united all the members of the house. That means: a Jewish family business was conducted over the interests of the states. That was already an "international syndicate"! In addition, moreover, it happens that the Rothschilds indeed married their daughters to European noble and princely descendants but, almost without exception, take Jewesses as wives. In this way, Jewish blood with the Jewish commercial spirit corroded the European peoples who found themselves in a sickness, but the Jewish race itself remained in its core mostly unmixed.

This must be premised to perceive that there is a conscious Jewish nation (today over 15 million souls), independent of their formal state citizenship; that this nation like all others bears a definite character; that this character consists in intellectual and material brokerage and has an effect today world-politically necessarily in such a way as always in history whenever it could have an effect. Only, it can do it today in a scope such as never before.

The present-day democractic governments are the consequences of elections. The elections are, in the first place, influenced by the press. The press is in the hands of rich stockholders. And these are today, in most countries, Jews. All parliamentarians are somehow dependent on, if not actually pushed forward by, all the parties of the "great democracies". Their masters are the Rothschilds, Warburgs, Schiffs, Kahns, Löbs, Speyers, Ellissens, Mendelssohns, Lamonds, Bleichröders, Strauß, etc. Dependent on Jewish finance are almost all the greats of this world.

The cited statement of the now dead Walter Rathenau is therefore to be considered as corresponding to the entire striving of the Jewish people. With deep understanding did his racial comrade, the former state-secretary, Dernburg, write on the occasion of Rathenau's nomination as "Minister of Reconstruction", in the *Berliner Tageblatt*:

"Rathenau is in the best sense international, because he comes from a world business, because he, in the course of a long life, has acquired many friendships among the foremost business men who however, in the final analysis, determine the fate of nations".

Those are the famous "three hundred among whom every person knows the other".

The final goal of a Jewish world-bank, of a Jewish world-syndicate, or however else one may call a financial system put together above all states, was therefore undoubtedly the goal of the stock-exchange lords of Paris, London, Berlin, New York, Petersburg, and Rome. If one observes the politics of the states from this standpoint, many incomprehensible things become comprehensible, many things seeming to be impenetrable previously suddenly clear as day. Once one accepted the law of gravitation as a theory and observed the course of the heavenly bodies. The path of a star was not explicable any longer on the basis of the observations upto that time. One had to assume one more invisible centre of power until the concerned star pressed into another path than that assumed on the basis of the calculations upto that time. Precise observations led to the discovery of a new planet. The latter presented the centre of power that had remained hidden until then.

In this way does it stand also with the present-day world-politics. Millions still naively employ only the powers of their calculation which are designated for them by our journalistic astrologers as the sole ones. And this calculation is never right even if one ever so learnedly adduces here all of history as a mid-wife to thoughtful political predictions. One speaks of "England", "France", etc. and forgets or fails to mention that neither England nor France nor any other state is to be judged still today on the basis of its historical national attitude alone, but always in relation to the new centre of power of the Jewish finance and its democratic-Marxist following.

There is today in the whole world no real national state, neither foreign politically nor internal politically. The "most excellent businessmen" who indeed "in the final analysis determine the fate of the nations" have constituted themselves already for a long time everywhere as a state within the state and at the same time a state above the states. They can, when it agrees with their calculation, apparently balance that with the national interests of individual states or state-groups and play the role of the greatest patriots, but are today already much too strong to sacrifice this calculation to the national requirements of the peoples who once took them in hospitably. Their power within every state naturally works immediately also foreign politically; the Jewish family-politics exerts for its part a foreign political pressure when the internal politics of a state threatens to become dangerous to the ruling financial and profiteering spirit.

On 10 June, 1895, the founder of political Zionism, Theodor Herzl,[72] wrote in his diary that "the next European war cannot harm us, but only promote us because all Jews will carry their property and possessions over in security; moreover we shall already therein speak at the conclusion of peace as money-lenders and aim at advantages of recognition by way of diplomacy". "[Carried] over in security" is today some two thirds of the entire gold of the world. In the treasures of the Wall Street Jews lies the blood of twelve million men of the white race transmuted into noble metal! That is the result of the most enormous world war, which has actually not harmed the Jews (overlooking some necessary sacrifice) but "only promoted" them. Entire villages, entire cities, are sunk in earthquakes. Entire provinces are destroyed and buried by poisonous grenades. The most beautiful monuments of ancient European culture have fallen there irrecoverably. An unnameable misery goes through hundreds of millions. But no nation has become free! Neither the betrayed nor the besieged, neither the victors nor their satellites have won the war, although all the field-greys, Poilu's and

---

72 Theodor Herzl (1860-1904) was a journalist and playwright and founder of political Zionism. Author of *Der Judenstaat* (1896) and *Altneuland* (1902) which envisioned a Jewish state in Palestine, Herzl organized the first Zionist Congress in Basel in 1897 as well as the five following Congresses.

Tommy's believed to be fighting for the freedom and international validity of their nation, and this idea first gave them the strength for their battle. All of them have been outrageously betrayed already *before the beginning* of the war, even though only today a few begin to open their eyes. The entire Jewish world press, which was concerned to nurture the discords already existing within different state-groups before the war, created such, or, if it lay in the plan, hindered a national defence as much as possible, does its best even today to retard the knowledge of the great world-betrayal, to stimulate in the lap of the peoples themselves the idea of class-warfare, or to distract their eyes from themselves to foreign political enemies. Enemies becoming dangerous, however, are sought to be lamed through financial "help".

This present-day almost exclusive rule of money was, as argued, secured already long before the war. The parliamentary elections in the western democracies were paid by the large banks, the press was conducted in a sense pleasant to the Jewish world-capitalism, and behind the soldiers of the different parties combating among themselves, in the final analysis, however, only the officer corps of the Jewish stock-exchange leadership itself was their leader, where the national interests of the different peoples were apparently promoted as well.

One may naturally not believe indeed that the Jewry has accepted the matter of the Entente with full enthusiasm. It has indeed supported this in the interest of its own business, but, inwardly, the Jew has remained in London or Paris as much a Jew as he was in Krakow or Warsaw. Perhaps not always consciously, but, in his instinctive influence, always.

It is, on the other hand, wrong when many people explain: if there were no Jews, peace would be secured. Obviously, the matters do not stand so simply. There were wars and there will be without Jews necessarily needing to incite them. But one thing should become clear to all: that peoples indeed can battle and should battle for their freedom and their right of existence, whereby however finally the situation existing for a long time must be removed that they strike one another for the benefit of one and the same laughing, racially foreign, third. Regardless of later possible discussions between nations, the leaders must gradually perceive that we, one and all, possess immediately a common foe: the Jewish red-golden international and its political dependence such as is embodied in certain professional parliamentarians and certain journalists.

It seems at first extraordinarily shrewd to strengthen the core of the disintegration in a still hostile neighbouring country and this were perhaps also politically clever: if the same pathogenic agents were not already settled in our own blood. For example, in 1917, some trains of

Bolshevist journeyed from Switzerland through Germany and Sweden to Russia, many ship-loads filled with the same sort of men came from the New York ghetto to Petersburg with the permission of the government of the United States and Great Britain. The seed indeed went over to Russia, but, as the receipt for that, the entire West has been infected with this pestilence. Germany has first of all to thank the victory of the Bolshevist Revolution in the east for the revolt of 9 November, 1918. With its present-day consequences. England has set the worm in the joints of its own house through the recognition of Soviet Judaea.[73] In France the Jew Léon Blum[74] tows alone with his henchmen a storm-proof guard in case the *bloc national* should no longer be viable and fit for use.

The "national Frenchmen" would therefore be glad, quite in vain, if in Germany Bolshevist uprisings should break out. If, as a result of them, the German Reich were to break apart, a French military dictatorship would perhaps be presumable, but in the long run not bearable even for the militarily strong, but financially too weak France. The foreign political failure however would mean catastrophe for the French general staff, and therewith however would conjure up the age of a Bastille-storming. One had to put forth similar considerations in London. One would presumably not do it yet, because it seems that different things must first clearly be revealed before their inner meaning is understood.

The western democracy has great statesmen as little as the German; almost all, no matter what they are called, have grown big through the Jewish stock-exchange and are pledged to it. In the "international private syndicate" they play an important but no decisive role. They have betrayed their peoples to the Hebrews, just as a Bethmann-Hollweg[75] did so with regard to the German nation and others continue it since then in strengthened measure. Like the "great democracies" even the small are drawn into the ring.

In short, as Harden-Witkowsky said in his *Future*[76] before the

---

73 cf. Rosenberg's essay `Soviet-Judäa'in *Kampf um die Macht*, 297-303.

74 Léon Blum (1872-1950) was the first Socialist Prime Minister of France (1936-37). Blum maintained political influence until 1948, when he was deputy Prime Minister.

75 Theobald von Bethmann Hollweg (1856-1921) was the son of a Frankfurt banker who served as Prussian Minister of the Interior in 1905 and became Reichskanzler and Prussian Minister President in 1909. Bethmann Hollweg was a moderate Conservative and the steps he took during the war made him unpopular with both right- and left-wing politicians. He finally resigned from his office in the face of Socialist opposition in 1917.

76 Maximilian Harden (born Felix Ernst Witkowski) (1861-1927) was a Jewish publicist and founder and editor of *Die Zukunft*. After 1918, Harden championed

Genoa Conference, "capitalism is becoming what Socialism appeared to be: international. Its calculation cannot be disturbed through borders and turnpikes, it estimates the nations beyond good and evil according to their creative performance, and confers its commissions to the suitable nation". That is the present federation in Europe: the stock-exchanges of London, Paris, and Moscow. Hemmed in by this political pressure, the masters breathe - insofar as they are non-Jewish - in Berlin and Rome.

If with the term, "private syndicate" the economic political side of the international idea were more emphasized, then the striving for a "federation of the nations" presents in many aspects the political side of the same thing. The "Workers' International" was an ideal behind which millions shuffled and, in general, even the world war was considered as a preliminary stage for this perceived world-tyranny. Thus did Trotski-Bronstein write shortly after the outbreak of the world war in his work, *War and the International*: "The war of 1914 signifies the wrecking of the national state as an independent economic system". It is a question of, it is indicated further, "the creation of a far more powerful fatherland and one more capable of resistance - the republican United States of Europe as the fundament of the United States of the World". The leaders of the International were therefore fully clear of the goal of their destructive activity. They were also, from their point of view, right when they designated the "national Philistines" as traitors in their Marxist camps. In the eyes of every true Bolshevist, the national idea signifies a crime against his "idea". This view came to expression very clearly in a well-known speech of the Marxist, Crispien, which he held on 11 January, 1922 at a Party Day: "We know no fatherland that is called Germany". And so deep have the German people already sunk that they helped such a man and his party to the Parliament!

The internationally-led world-republic was, further, the expressed goal of the Freemasonic secret unions, even when so much of these seemed national chauvinistic and considered the leadership of the striven-for world-state differently than their fraternal organisation in the neighbouring country.

In 1889, the centennial celebration of the French Revolution took place in Paris. At this spoke Brother Frankolin of the Grand Orient and explained that, for all empires which did not yet have a 1789, this day must come: "This day is not far any longer. That is the day which we are looking at. Then all great lodges and Grand Orients will find themselves

---

the Socialist cause. A few days after Rathenau's murder, Harden was also wounded in an assassination attempt by Conservatives and had to flee to Switzerland.

in a world fraternization. That is the brilliant ideal of the future which hovers before us". In 1900, the inter-state Freemasonic Congress established anew the basic idea of this political world organisation. The president of the same, Bourceret, closed his speech with the words: "The call, 'Long live the World-Republic!' will soon no longer be platonic". Precisely in this way did the other speakers speak.

It would lead too far away to go into the details more closely. It is a fact that these Freemasonic Congresses were the expression of will of those forces which today determine the world-politics. And with the same necessity with which the Jewry penetrated into the world economy, it was able to empower itself also with the leadership of the Freemasonry. The Jew, settled everywhere, everywhere different and yet the same, formed the natural strong cement of all internationally bound societies and was obviously eagerly concerned for centuries to strengthen this attitude and, therewith, its influence.

So it was not surprising if, after the war, the "Peace" Conferences as well as the other international "Reparations" conventions indeed revealed non-Jewish representatives, and yet these had, one and all, Jewish friends or companions: Lloyd George the Jew Philipp Sassoon, Balfour Anthony Rothschild, the French representatives brought the Jew Mantoux, Italy was represented for a long time by the Jew Schanzer, Germany by Rathenau. From the side of America the Jewish financial kings, Baruch, Kahn, Warburg, toured the countries. Soviet "Russia" dispatched the Radeks, Rakowiskys, Litwinow-Finkelsteins, etc. Thanks to ever new loans and taxes and external debts, all nations have become obliged to tributes with regard to private financial concerns and syndicates. This financial rule enslaving all the nations has become the most disgraceful, but undeniably most important fact of world-politics. To shake this off from it and to give to every nation its most characteristic possession, the possibility of racial renewal, is what the present-day world-battle signifies.

This battle is played out today already in all fields. An instinctive, primally powerful battle declaration is announced against the world- and political view which saw the light in 1789, at the same time, however, against that other which values the national culture as such only as a stage of development that is to be overcome. The Communists preach to us a world-revolution. Now, this world-revolution is "on the way", but, to be sure, in a quite different way than the apostles of Lenin accepted it. Whereas Communism represents, world-politically, the last, cramped, spiritually empty throe of the masses sceptical of the Liberal-international world-view (as regards the following) and at the same time the Jewish attempt at the destruction of Europe (as regards the leadership), today there emerges for the first time once again a new ideal as a power going through all the strata of the people. The old nationalism was not capable of combating the Bolshevist world-revolution, it was itself capitalistically infected, often closely related in its leadership in all states in a Jewish way, and had forgotten that the external power should not be a goal in itself but a means of the general defence of the people. The old Moltke[77] said at the end of his life: "Now we provide for the soldiers only the businesses of the stock-exchange". Thus 1914 became the beginning of the stock-exchange-Bolshevist war of destruction against the white race with the help of the European peoples themselves.

From the chaos, however, from need and shame, has emerged the racial idea against the international idea. The victory of this ideal in all fields signifies the real world-revolution of the twentieth century.

This racial ideal signifies the recognition of the idea of power and still not imperialism. The first, insofar as the idea of power presents nothing else but the expression of the internal racial-national life will and the attempt to fight for the natural self-development, if necessary with one's life. Not imperialism: for, precisely from the conscious recognition of the actual personality-worth and of the special character of one's own people - in the wider sense: of the race - follows also the actual evaluation of other genuine racial characteristics. The manner and way in which, for example, the 19th century brought to China the opium compulsion and conducted exploitation in all parts of the world is a crime which can be avenged still in a frightful way. For, one who has eyes to see perceives that the yellow and the black races can arm themselves for a coming world war. The European states have not felt obligations with regard to the other races, but observed their colonies mostly from the standpoint of the possibility of economic exploitation. Just as the economic leaders did it even in Europe and, therewith, prepared the ground for the decomposition of the nations. If the racial law succeeds in coming to an outbreak in Europe, this will have an effect also world-politically. Germany for the Germans, China for the Chinese, that becomes the world-political view from the racial conception of the state. The European racial pride would not be affected thereby but, for the first time, awakened to true consciousness after it has been contaminated until now by the business mentality. For, not unjustly did the cultured man of the East often see a barbarian in the European. The realization of the racial idea means therefore: victory of the national consciousness and of the idea of the state over economic interests and the race-less financial

---

77 Helmuth von Moltke (1848-1916), Chief of the General Staff who resigned after the German defeat at the Battle of the Marne.

dictatorship of individuals.

Only from that is produced real striving for social justice. For, the latter can be produced and carried out only by the state, which is master and not servant; which, further, has grasped that the racial work-power and the life-will can be secured and maintained only through social justice. Because there has been no real national state, therefore all talk of justice on the part of the democratic parliamentarians was nothing but lies and deception. For, the capitalistic democracy could live only on the misery of the peoples. It grew from speculation and corruption, from exploitation and racial disgrace. Social justice as the result of the racial idea would mean inevitably the death of the Marxist-democratic century.

A new idea emerges from the darkness and suddenly throws a quite different light on the past, present and future. An age sinks thereby into chaos and desperation. And new spiritual power rises against the chaos. Like a stream does it proceed over the world: from the Indian Ocean, over Egypt's deserts and the Turkish Asia Minor, there moves a similar spiritual current as has already rushed forth in Italy, in Germany and will also find its expansion in other states. The phenomenal forms of the racial idea are naturally different. In many places it will not be able to be realized clearly through lack of racially adequately strong men. But undeniable is the will to freedom, of the self, of the people, of the race.

From the international bank-state of the Jewish world-stock-exchange it is important to release or chisel out one state after another, until that usurious structure collapses which sucks the marrow of all the nations, and makes its power from the strength of others.

We are not dreamers and preach no "world peace", and no eternal fraternization. But no matter what the future may bring - we strive with all the strength of our racial internal political and external political liberation from the immoral profiteering-state; liberation of our European racial consciousness with regard to the other races of the globe; the victory of an aristocratic idea over the sordid commercial mentality of the age that passes away at present. That is the world-battle of today, the world-revolution of tomorrow, the war of which we do not know when it will be ended, which however must be fought through, if Germany and the entire old Europe should not decay in the morass as so many peoples of ancient history did.

That however a new conception of the world and the state could be born shows that the spiritual powers are still alive in us. It is important to listen to them, it is important to strengthen them, till the day of victory.

"United States of Europe?", *Völkischer Beobachter*, 13/14 September 1925.[78]

In the last months, parallel with the propaganda for the "League of Nations", also the activity of the so-called "Pan-European Society" has been strengthening itself. At the same time, different press organs set forth questionnaires among politicians and writers on how they considered the so-called "United States of Europe". Thus the *Neue Wiener Journal* set up in this way such an inquiry and requested a series of well-known personalities of all states for information regarding their opinion on the following questions:

1. Do you consider the creation of the United States of Europe as necessary?

2. Do you consider the realization of the United States of Europe as possible?

To these questions the French Finance Minister, Caillaux, replied that the patriotism of the 20th century would merge with Europeanism. The "Easter day of the European union" will come, it will come even as fatally as there are physical laws. Ignaz Seipel, the former Federal Chancellor of Austria, hopes for the same thing and wishes a "revision of the conception of the state" in general! Similarly did Anton Svelah, the Ministerial President of Czechoslovakia, express himself.

Jakob Lippowitz, the Jewish editor of the *Neue Wiener Journal* explains: the border-posts had proven to be true torture posts for every European state citizen. Similarly do Maximilian Harden, Albert Einstein, Alfred Kerr, and obviously Dr. Gerhart Hauptmann, Heinrich Mann and Dr. Thomas Mann, express themselves!

As one sees, an entire series of personalities are agreed on the catch-word of the United States of Europe. Yet it is naturally clear that most of them understand something quite different thereby. Mr. Lippowitz and his consorts surely think of a single Jewish private syndicate, just as Walter Rathenau also indeed imagined it. To this then all the states would have had to be joined. Ignaz Seipel, however, dreams surely of the mediaeval rule of the Church, and the others pursue their very real foreign political goals thereby.

But, whatever the motivating reasons of the individuals may be, the fact of a strong movement for a somehow articulated European union lies ahead and we therefore have to tackle this problem and explain our attitude to it.

Doubtless an awakening is being manifested in the whole world.

---

78 Reprinted in A. Rosenberg, *Blut und Ehre*, pp.267-69.

The awakening of the Near and Far East, and indeed on a racial background, is openly visible, and even the black continent has begun in a similar way to make its claims known. Only a fool can believe that this extra-European pressure does not demand also a common European attitude. This awakening of the Near and Far East is the answer to the exploitative economy and the disintegrating influences which the commercial Europe dragged after its political conquests to India and China. But this unlimited exploitative economy and exploitative politics has promoted all bad instincts not only in the colonies and colony-like countries but also unchained them in Europe itself, where they are systematically stirred up further by shrewd politicians. The present-day propaganda for the "United States of Europe" which originates from the circles of the stock-exchange and the Jewish press means nothing more than a logical continuation of this same exploitative economy sanctioned by a politically strengthened union. It is therefore obvious that we stand in strong opposition to this new betrayal. It is, on the other hand, a fact that the foreign political knowledge begins to awaken everywhere, that a reciprocal warring of the European nations means also the end of every national culture. This awakening feeling of a foreign political European solidarity is today exploited and falsified by the same political people to whom all the nations are indebted for their present-day misery. The "United States of Europe" would have to be rejected by us along with all others, solely from the basis that such a type as the half-Asiatic Count Coudenhove-Kalergi[79] is their chief announcer. The latter preaches, instead of attaching himself to the organic, the race and nationality, absolute racial mixture and is therewith to be observed as the new harbinger of the downfall of Europe.

Still, the knowledge of the necessity of a foreign politically closed Europe stands beyond question, even though it must bring along with it an entire series of burdensome problems. But one must consider that when we stand before an either-or - destruction of the West or securing of Europe in the world - ways must also be found to attain to this goal. At the top stands a demand without whose fulfilment all is in vain: the elimination of the Jews from all the states of Europe. This in turn can be only the result of an awakening of the racial feeling, of a new idea of the state, and of a new conception of the economic life.

---

79 cf. p.113 above.

"Europe's Revolution", *Völkischer Beobachter*, 12 May, 1940.[80]

On 10 May, 1940, the National Socialistic Revolution and, with it, the National Socialistic Reich has entered the decisive stage of European preservation and world-political ratification. When we saw in 1933 the powers hostile to us in the Reich brought down, we knew that they indeed did not represent German phenomena, but were essentially in their leadership the extended arm of international powers. We saw also how much the traitors of Germany driven from there bound themselves immediately with their old spiritual comrades and contract-givers in Paris and London, in Vienna and in Prague, and called forth to life once again a common agitation against Germany. We knew that the Jewish high finance had declared war against Germany with all its subject powers, for this Germany had first of all, and for all peoples, visibly broken the dictatorship of the Jewish stock-exchange lords, driven all corrupters of German culture and the German past, and these knew only too well that in great crises even recovery may infect. In these years, the enemies of the German Reich must have ascertained that even in other states men actually existed who awoke from the Jewish-democratic hypnosis and began to wish to change even the fate of their own country for the better. What in the beginning still paralysed the powers of decision to attack us was the hope that Adolf Hitler would not be finished with those problems which the earlier power-holders who had run from there had left behind for us. They knew what a degeneration was intellectually instituted, they knew what economic and social chaos existed in Germany; they knew what hatred had arisen once again in Germany in every class and believed that the National Socialistic Revolution would be ruined by mismanagement after half a year, at most after a year, and that then an attack could be undertaken without risk!

Here lies the decisive failure of thought of all those who stand today raging and yet inwardly powerless before the power of the German Reich raised high. We National Socialists are of the conviction that the Churchills and Reynauds are plucking out their last hairs and heap themselves with complaints that they did not attack us already in 1933 as they had wished. The fact, however, that they abstained from that lies not only in the former conviction that we would "be ruined by mismanagement", but also in the clear knowledge that their peoples were not to be called forth to a war without a visible reason, that an occasion

---

80 Reprinted in A. Rosenberg, *Tradition und Gegenwart*, pp.443-51.

visible to all was not visible and that the social problems themselves occupied them daily whereby it seemed impossible to lead the nations exhausted by fighting once again to war without a reason perceptible to all.

In this great political process from 1933 to 1940, the single decisive fact is proved that, in spite of all screaming about democracy and humanity, the peoples could no longer, in increasing measure, believe in these "ideals". Once, in the age of the French Revolution, it may have swept along the masses because this generation was filled with hatred against the absolutist regime of the 18th century. At that time, the masses united at first this hatred against the decayed and corrupt present, they celebrated enthusiasts and dreamers in the conviction of leading in a "new, better, world". The first revolutionary surge collapsed soon into itself, and the 19th century meant the progressing degeneration of the enthusiastic ideas of the 18th century. Fraternity turned into the rule of money; humanity turned into the most brutal economic imperialism which the world had ever seen; the consideration of men for one another turned into the systematic physical poisoning of entire peoples through opium wars and calico trade. Blooming industries of old cultured nations were destroyed by the trash from Manchester - and not only from Manchester - and over all there triumphed then only one power over all other ideas: profit!

Within this process which received a doubtlessly also grandiose façade through a colossal development of technology, millions upon millions were socially stunted and the more these powers were concentrated from below, the more did the capitalistic trust- and financial interests merge together. What we experienced later as social desperation even in Germany and what smouldered under the surface in England exactly as in France are the immediate results of this unscrupulous economic imperialism. Once, in 1919, in Versailles, it had the power of the entire world in its hands, but it did not bring world-peace but a world-exploitation of the greatest degree, did not bring national justice but the most stupid anti-European dictatorship that anti-European corrupt brains could ever have thought of.

Here lies the essence of the great discussion which the present-day world-political regulation has assumed. England, incapable of grasping a new age, has established its politics only in an extra-European way, and established all dealings on the mainland of Europe only from the security of its *imperium* outside the European continent. France, petty, misguided and impotent, could not separate itself from its old outdated idea of dismembering Germany. Both political efforts, if they had succeeded, would have had to lead to a powerlessness of Europe and the partition of the most diverse powers of the European mainland. Europe would have been present, at most, as a contentless hinterland of the British insular empire, that is, that power which once determined the fate of the world would have been dissolved and been made incapable of action for coming ages.

Beyond all other feelings and thoughts, therefore, the National Socialistic Revolution has united the 80 million Germans in a great Reich, at the same time, however, also introduced once again the unification of Europe. It may be that, in the states of the north or of the south-east, one considers this great phenomenon still with mistrust, indeed in places with rejection, but if the leaders of these nations now ponder more deeply on the fate standing before us, then however they must perceive some facts finally. The blockade by England shows that the possibility was actually present that hundreds of millions of Europeans saw their fate lying suddenly in the hands of a single enormous world-economic undertaking called the British Empire. The finance from London and the fleet politics led by it had the power to cut off entire groups of people from the necessary means of life and powers of existence, to destroy them economically, to drive them against one another politically and therewith to make the profit-interests of the Jewish-English stock-exchange the law of Europe. The hypnosis of this possibility was so strong that only few could think of a change of this situation. Above all, there was no one who had led together the peoples of the north and of the south-east in Europe under such an all-European idea. Here now the German Reich has entered into its old European mission and shows in the 20th century that the attitude of the German Reich in the early Middle Ages was no accident but a necessity, a necessity not only because the Germanic-Teutonic power developed itself into fullest elevation, but also because of the knowledge that if Europe wished to preserve its independence, this was to be made possible only through an organizing power on the European continent itself.

The present-day 80 million people of Germany awakened once again to its pride could not satisfy itself with a possibility of the constriction of its entire existence through an extra-European commercial power. It has smoothened, as we all know, through its speaker, Adolf Hitler, all paths to an understanding both with the English and with the French. The representatives of these nations have found open doors in Germany, one has over and over again opened to them a European cooperative work, naturally under the self-explanatory condition that, just as Germany was ready to observe the life-necessities of the others, it also must at the same time insist on the demand of seeing the possibility of existence and free life of the great German nation secured. Nevertheless one has always returned in London and in Paris to the most petty, backward, intrigue politics. Not a single great man was present there worthy of being the partner of Adolf Hitler or Mussolini; a great hour found pathetic dwarfs. One blabbered out the old words which one had pronounced under quite different circumstances in past centuries; one still stammered something about ideals of mankind and humanity and had, however, not a single ounce of true humanity to bestow.

In view of this fact which becomes increasingly clearer, the German Reich has drawn the internal and external consequences and no one has watched so indefatigably over the strength and honour of Germany as the Führer. What therefore has explained the war today is the economic-capitalistic 19th century led by the Jewish-British greed for profit and what stands on Germany's side is the awakened 20th century! As a bridge between the two ages lies the gap of the entire Versailles system.

The ideas which march today with the standards of the German Reich are the ideas of a rising new age against the crumbling, worn out ways of speech of hypocritical officials of international finance. What National Socialism and its world-view mean for Germany we old National Socialists know as well as the entire generation of young men who have emerged, from a great awakened instinct, for the defence of the new Reich. But what the National Socialistic Revolution means for all nations, for all of Europe, will be tested and hardened in this war. It means, even when many statesmen do not yet wish to perceive it, the liberation of all European nations from the nightmare of a finance-piratical system which was until now strong enough to develop from its hand death-threatening powers of destruction.

It means that the European peoples proclaim together under the common German battle vanguard the freedom of the entire European continent from extra-European profit interests.

It means that all these nations, forced by the English blockade, must reconsider their entire economic policy, their entire export policy, and therewith their entire political regime.

It means that the peoples of the south-east, along with the peoples of the northern territory, must set up the most precise investigations on how their reciprocal self-maintenance is possible without assistance of extra-European powers. It means that here the German Reich comes into appearance power-politically as the decisive reloading point of these living-spaces.

It means that this balance, which lies in the life-interest of all these mentioned peoples, will be possible solely through the decisive political and military weight of the German central Europe.

The nations will in future in this way, perhaps often under

temporary renunciation of customary enjoyments, never see their immediate existence threatened and then, of course not in the sense of a large capitalistic League of Nations, come to a common European co-operation. There is in life not only the so-called unlimited battle for existence, but also, scientifically expressed, a so-called symbiosis, that is, a commonality of work for the guaranteeing of quite different types and peoples. That is doubtless the new European trend which today begins to be fulfilled in a great destiny, and we are of the firm conviction that here the National Socialistic German Reich is the pioneer of this new European freedom and new order. (The coal agreement between Germany and Italy is an example of this European solidarity). We are of the firm conviction that these ideas will gradually be taken possession of by many other nations and that these will be strong enough to recover from the English sickness called stock-exchange democracy.

Therefore the war, which now has begun, visible to all the world, on 10 May, 1940, is a revolutionary war of the greatest scope. The National Socialistic Revolution which saved Germany has thus become the vanguard of the preservation of the life-rights of the entire European continent. It strikes down the life-hostile decayed pieces of an economic imperialistic age and lays with the stride of its armies and the power of its ideals firm foundations for a new cohabitation of the European peoples.

That which was thought of for us in order to destroy us: the British blockade, had logically to be extended even to other nations which had done as little for England as we had. The Jewish-English imperialism had to threaten even their life-nerves, and for that reason has the march of the Germans to the north become the rescue of the entire living-space of the northern peoples for the future. Therefore the exchange of goods with the south-east means the stabilising of the national economies of these peoples of the Danube territory in opposition to the credits of the banks and stock-exchanges of Paris and London which suck up these peoples. The 20th century has emerged visibly to the entire world on 10 May, 1940. An old age sinks under the march of the German army, and the entire German people stands today in the consciousness of leading for ever their own battle for freedom, at the same time, however, also in the consciousness of bearing on their strong shoulders, with the Idea of it, a great mission, for coming centuries, for the entire sacred continent.

Bibliography

I. Primary Sources
(Included here are the major political and philosophical works of the four authors presented in this edition)

a. Paul de Lagarde

Deutsche Schriften, Göttingen: Dietrich, 1878-81, 1886. [The essays in this volume are:
"Konservativ?"
"Ueber das Verhältnis des deutschen Staates zu Theologie, Kirche und Religion".
"Drei Vorreden".
"Diagnose".
"Ueber die gegenwärtige Lage des deutschen Reichs".
"Zum Unterrichtsgesetze".
"Die Religion der Zukunft".
"Die Stellung der Religionsgesellschaften im Staate".
"Noch einmal zum Unterrichtsgesetze".
"Die Reorganization des Adels".
"Die Finanzpolitik Deutschlands".
"Die graue Internationale".
"Programm für die konservative Partei Preußens".
"Ueber die Klage, daß der deutschen Jugend der Idealismus fehle".
"Die nächsten Pflichten deutscher Politik".]
Mittheilungen, 4 vols., Göttingen: Dietrich, 1884-91.

b: Constantin Frantz

Die Philosophie der Mathematik: zugleich ein Beitrag zur Logik und Naturphilosophie, Leipzig: H. Hartung, 1842.

Grundsätze des wahren und wirklichen absoluten Idealismus, Berlin: W. Hermes, 1843.

Über den Atheismus mit besonderer Bezugnahme auf Ludwig Feuerbach, Berlin: W. Hermes, 1844.

Vorschule zur Physiologie der Staaten, Berlin: F. Schneider, 1859.

Quid faciamus nos, 1858.

Untersuchungen über das europäische Gleichgewicht, Berlin: F. Schneider, 1859.

Über Gegenwart und Zukunft der preussischen Verfassung, Halberstadt: R. Frantz, 1846.

Drei und dreissig Sätze vom Deutschen Bunde, Berlin: F. Schneider, 1861.

Kritik aller Parteien, Berlin: F. Schneider, 1862.

Die Quelle alles Übels: Betrachtungen über die preussische Verfassungskrisis, Stuttgart: J.G. Cotta, 1863.

Die Wiederherstellung Deutschland's, Berlin: F. Schneider, 1865.

Die Naturlehre des Staates als Grundlage aller Staatswissenschaft, Leipzig: C.F. Winter, 1870.

Das neue Deutschland, beleuchtet in Briefen an einen preussischen Staatsmann, Leipzig: Rossberg, 1871.

Die Religion des Nationalliberalismus, Leipzig: Rossberg, 1872.

Literarisch-politische Aufsätze, nebst einem Vorwort über die Verdienste des Fürsten Bismarck, und einem Nachwort über deutsche Politik, München: M. Huttler, 1876.

Deutsche Antwort auf die orientalische Frage, Leipzig: E. Bidder, 1877.

Der Untergang der alten Parteien der Zukunft, Berlin: M.A. Niendorf, 1878.

Der Föderalismus als das leitende Princip für die sociale, staatliche und internationale Organization, unter besonderer Bezugnahme auf Deutschland, Mainz: F. Kirchheim, 1879.

Schelling's positive Philosophie, 3 vols., Köthen: P. Schettler, 1879-90.

Die sociale Steuerreform, Mainz: F. Kirchheim, 1881.

Die Weltpolitik, unter besonderer Bezugnahme auf Deutschland, 3 vols., Chemnitz: E. Schmeitzner, 1882-83.

c. Edgar Julius Jung

Die Herrschaft der Minderwertigen. Ihr Zerfall und ihre Ablösung.
Berlin, Verlag Deutsche Rundschau, 1927.
Die Herrschaft der Minderwertigen. Ihr Zerfall und ihre Ablösung.
Berlin, Verlag Deutsche Rundschau, 1929/30.
The Rule of the Inferiour, translated, with an Introduction and Notes, by
Alexander Jacob. Lewiston, NY: The Edwin Mellen Press, 1995.
Föderalismus aus Weltanschauung, Berlin und Leipzig, J. Schweitzer
Verlag, 1931.
(ed.) *Deutsche über Deutschland. Die Stimme des unbekannten
Politikers*, München, Albert Langen-Georg Müller Verlag, 1932.
Sinndeutung der deutschen Revolution, Oldenburg, Gerhard Stalling,
1933.

d. Alfred Rosenberg

Die Spur des Juden im Wandel der Zeiten, München: Deutscher
Volksverlag, 1920.
*Das Verbrechen der Freimaurerei: Judentum, Jesuitismus, deutsches
Christentum*, München: Hoheneichen Verlag, 1921.
(ed.) *Das Parteiprogramm: Wesen, Grundsätze und Ziele der NSDAP*,
München: F. Eher Nachfolger, 1922.
Die Protokolle der Weisen von Zion und die jüdische Weltpolitik,
München: Deutscher Volksverlag, 1923.
*Die internationale Hochfinanz als Herrin der Arbeiterbewegung in allen
Ländern*, München: E. Boepple, 1925.
Der Zufkunftsweg einer deutschen Aussenpolitik, München: F. Eher
Nachfolger, 1927.
*Houston Stewart Chamberlain als Verkünder und Begründer einer
deutschen Nation*, München: H. Bruckmann, 1927.
*Der Sumpf: Querschnitte durch das `Geistes'-leben der November-
Demokratie*, München: F. Eher Nachfolger, 1930.
Freimaureische Weltpolitik im Lichte der kritischen Forschung,
München: F. Eher Nachfolger, 1929.
Der Mythus des 20. Jahrhunderts, München: Hoheneichen Verlag, 1930.
*Das Wesensgefüge des Nationalsozialismus: Grundlagen der deutschen
Wiedergeburt*, München: F. Eher Nachfolger, 1932.
*An die dunkelmänner unserer Zeit: eine Antwort auf die Angriffe gegen
den `Mythus des 20. Jahrhunderts'*, München: Hoheneichen, 1935.

Protestantische Rompilger: der Verrat an Luther und der `Mythus des 20. Jahrhunderts, München: Hoheneichen Verlag, 1937.
Der staatsfiendliche Zionismus, München: F. Eher Nachfolger, 1938.
Novemberköpfe, München: F. Eher Nachfolger, 1939.

Collected Essays:

Blut und Ehre: ein Kampf für deutsche Wiedergeburt. Reden und Aufsätze von 1919-1933, ed. Thilo von Trotha, München: F. Eher Nachfolger, 1934.
Gestaltung der Idee. Reden und Aufsätze von 1933-1935, ed. T. von Trotha, München: F. Eher Nachfolger, 1936.
Kampf um die Macht. Aufsätze von 1921-1932, ed. T. von Trotha, München: F. Eher Nachfolger, 1937.
Tradition und Gegenwart. Reden und Aufsätze, 1936-1940, ed. K. Rüdiger, München: F. Eher Nachfolger, 1941.
Schriften aus den Jahren 1917-1921, ed. A. Bäumler, München: Hoheneichen, 1944.

II. Secondary Literature
(This is a selected list)

Boehm, Max Hildebert   *Europa Irredenta*, Berlin: Reimer Hobbing, 1923.
Blüher, Hans *Secessio Judaica*, Berlin: Der weisse Ritter Verlag, 1922.
Gesammelte Auafsätze, Jena: E. Diederichs, 1991.
Cecil, Robert *The myth of the master-race: Alfred Rosenberg and Nazi ideology*, London: Batford, 1972.
Chamberlain, Houston Stewart *Politische Ideale*, München: F. Bruckmann, 1915.
Political Ideals, tr. with an Introduction by Alexander Jacob, Hillsboro, West Virginia: National Vanguard Books, 1995.
Dawson, W.H. *The German Empire 1867-1914 and the unity movement*, 2 vols., N.Y.: The Macmillan Co., 1919.
Droz, Jacques   *L'Europe centrale: évolution historique de l'idée de `Mitteleuropa'*, Paris: Payot, 1960.
Dühring, Eugen *Die Judenfrage als Racen-, Sitten- und Culturfrage: mit einer welgeschichtlichen   Antwort*, Karlsruhe: H. Reuther, 1881 (2nd. ed. 1881, 3rd. ed. 1886).
Ehmer, Manfred *Constantin Frantz: die politische Gedankenwelt eines*

Klasskers des Föderalismus, Rheinfelden: Schäuble Verlag, 1988.

Favrat, Jean *La pensée de Paul de Lagarde (1827-1891): Contribution à l'étude des rapports de la réligion et de la politique dans le nationalisme et le conservatisme allemande au XIXème siècle*, Paris, 1979.

Härtle, Heinrich *Großdeutschland. Traum und Tragödie: Rosenbergs Kritik am Hitlerismus*, München: H. Härtle, 1970.

Héraud, Guy *Les principes du fédéralisme et la fédération européene: contribution à la théorie juridique du fédéralisme*, Paris: Presses d'Europe, 1968.

Hitler, Adolf *Hitlers zweites Buch: ein Dokument aus dem Jahr 1928*, ed. G.L. Weinberg, Stuttgart: Deutsche Verlaganstalt, 1961.

Hitler's secret book, tr. S. Attanasio, N.Y.: Grove Press, 1961.

Jahnke, Helmut Edgar Julius Jung: *Ein Konservativer Revolutionär zwischen Tradition und Moderne*, Pfaffenweiler: Centaurus Verlagsgesellschaft, 1998.

Jenschke, Bernhard *Zur Kritik der konservative-revolutionären Ideologie in der Weimarer Republik. Weltanschauung und Politik bei Edgar Julius Jung*, München, 1971.

Jones, Larry Eugene "Edgar Julius Jung: The conservative revolution in theory and practice", *Central European History*, 21 (1988), 142-174

"The limits of collaboration: Edgar Jung, Herbert von Bose, and the origins of the conservative resistance to Hitler, 1933-34", in *Between Reform, Reaction, and Resistance: Studies in the history of German conservatism from 1789 to 1945*, Oxford and Providence, R.I., 1993, 465-501.

Jones, L.E. and Retallack (ed.), *Between Reform, Reaction, and Resistance: Studies in the History of German Conservatism from 1789 to 1945*, Oxford and Providence, R.I., 1993.

Lougey, Robert *Paul de Lagarde, 1827-1891: a study of radical conservatism in Germany*, Cambridge, MA: HUP, 1962.

Mann, Thomas *Betrachtungen eines Unpolitischen*, Berlin: S. Fischer Verlag, 1918.

Reflections of a nonpolitical man, tr. W.D. Morris, N.Y.: Frederick Ungar, 1983.

Mantino, Suzanne *Die `Neue Rechte' in der `Grauzone' zwischen Rechtsextremismus und Konservatismus*, Frankfurt am Main: Peter Lang, 1992.

Matz, Adolph *Herkunft und Gestalt der Adam Müllerschen Lehre von Staat und Kunst*, Philadelphia: Univ. of Pennsylvania, 1937.

Meinecke, Friedrich *Weltbürgertum und Nationalstaat*, München: R. Oldenbourg, 1907.

Cosmopolitanism and the national state, tr. R.B. Kimber, Princeton:

PUP, 1970.

Meyer, H.C. *Mitteleuropa in German thought and action*, The Hague: Martinus Nijhoff, 1955.

Müller, Adam *Die Elemente der Staatskunst*, ed. J. Baxa, 2 vols., Jena: G. Fischer, 1922.

Müller, J.B. *Konservatismus und Außenpolitik*, Berlin: Rotbuch Verlag, 1990.

Naumann, Friedrich *Mitteleuropa*, Berlin: G. Reimer, 1916.

Niewyk, Donald "Solving the `Jewish problem': continuity and change in German antisemitism, 1871-1945", *Leo Baeck Institute Yearbook* 35 (1990), pp.335-370.

Paller, Heinz v. *Der großdeutsche Gedanke: seine Entstehung und Entwicklung bis zur Gegenwart*, Leipzig: Historisch-politischer Verlag Rudolf Hofstetter, 1

Riemeck, Renate *Mitteleuropa: Bilanz eines Jahrhunderts*, Freiburg im Breislau, Verlag Die Kommenden, 1981.

Roemheld, Lutz *Integraler Federalismus: Modell für Europa - ein Weg zur personalen Gruppengesellschaft*, München, 1977.

Integral Federalism: Model for Europe - a way towards a personal group society, tr. Hazel Bongert, Frankfurt am Main: Peter Lang, 1990.

Rogger, H. and Weber, E. *The European Right: a historical profile*, Berkeley: Univ. of California Press, 1965.

Schmid, Thomas *Staatsbegräbnis: von ziviler Gesellschaft*, Berlin: Rotbuch Verlag, 1990.

Schnur, Roman "Mitteleuropa in preußischen Sicht: Constantin Frantz", in *Mitteleuropa: Spuren der Vergangenheit - Perspektiven der Zukunft*, Innsbruck: Universität Innsbruck, 1987, pp.37-42.

Schwedhelm, Karl (ed.) *Propheten des Nationalismus*, München: List Verlag, 1969.

See, Klaus von *Die Ideen von 1789 und die Ideen von 1914: Völkisches Denken in Deutschland zwischen französischer Revolution und erstem Weltkrieg*, Frankfurt am Main, 1975.

Scruton, Roger *The meaning of Conservatism*, London: The Macmillan Press, 1984.

Stamm, Eugen *Ein berühmter Unberühmter: neue Studien über Konstantin Frantz und den Föderalismus*, Konstanz: Curt Weller, 1948.

Stapel, Wilhelm *Der christliche Staatsmann*, Hamburg: Hanseatische Verlag, 1932.

Stern, Jacques `Mitteleuropa' von Leibniz biz Naumann über List und Frantz, Planck und Lagarde*, Stuttgart: Deutscher Verlagsanstalt, 1917.

Sunic, Tomislav *Against democracy and equality: the European New Right*, N.Y.: Peter Lang, 1990.

Voyenne, Bernard *Histoire de l'idée fédéraliste*, 3 vols., Paris: Presses d'Europe, 1976-81.
Whisker, James *The social, political, and religious thought of Alfred Rosenberg: an interpretive essay*, Washington, D.C.: University Press of America, 1982.

General Index